The New Life of God in the Soul of Man

The New Life of God in the Soul of Man

AN INTERPRETATION OF
HENRY SCOUGAL'S CLASSIC

~

John D. Gillespie

Myrrh
Books
Overland Park, Kansas

The New Life of God in the Soul of Man
An Interpretation of Henry Scougal's Classic
John D. Gillespie
© 2017 John D. Gillespie
Myrrh Books, Overland Park, Kansas
ISBN: 1548437409
ISBN-13: 9781548437404

Holy Bible, New International Version® Anglicized, NIV® Copyright © 1979, 1984, 2011 by Biblica, Inc.®
Used by permission. All rights reserved worldwide.
Romans 8:1 – All Wrongs Reversed. The author happily grants permission for any part of this work to be reproduced, within context, and with the sincere desire to promote the Glory of God.
Special thanks to my sister, Nell Riechers, and to my wife, Tessa, for their tireless work in editing and preparing this manuscript.
Library of Congress Control Number: 2017911004

Foreword

By Jake Barreth

〜

A SINGLE, FLICKERING LIGHTBULB SWAYED silently overhead as 25 Haitian pastors, packed shoulder to shoulder, stared wide-eyed at the speaker.

"It's a sin to be boring!" Echoing off the cinderblock walls, these opening remarks ping-ponged around for a few seconds before landing squarely, like a slap, on my forehead. Every eye widened in anticipation of the next sentence, "What you think about when you think about Jesus is the most important thing about you!" "How can a Christian possibly be bored with Jesus?" "How could a pastor possibly teach a boring message about Jesus?"

It's 10 AM at All-In-One Church in Dargout, Haiti, and already the temperature outside the classroom is soaring into the high eighties. … Day one of a three-day pastor training/equipping conference. Morning rays of light begin to streak through the ventilated block wall scorching everything in their path. Pastors squeeze into tight rows of shared desk space as beads of perspiration cling precariously to their brows. The air shifts. A slight breeze cuts through the musty room causing every neck to crane in its direction.

Ordinarily, these conditions would make for a difficult learning environment; however, today every eye is locked in as John Gillespie begins his - very non-boring - adventure with Jesus.

I met John briefly a few weeks earlier. He had been introduced to me by a long-time supporter of The Global Orphan Project (GO Project) where I serve as the Director of International Orphan Care. After hearing that I was looking for someone to help provide theological training to GO Project's pastor partners in Haiti, an introduction was made. A few weeks later I found myself sitting in a classroom listening to John excitedly teaching through chapters of Wayne Grudem's *Systematic Theology*, to dozens of Haitian Pastors. Over the next few days I learned John and I share many things in common. We both spent an extended period living in the UK, John's 26 years to my 16. We share a deep love for playing guitar and a respect for classic literature (especially Charles Dickens). John's quick-witted, dry sense of humor kept me on my toes as we would joust slyly in retort to each other's good-natured insults. He would razz me about my numerous tattoos, while I would zing him about how it must be nice to not have to worry about packing shampoo on account of his exceptionally sparse hairline.

I left Haiti feeling that John was a good friend, a man whom I deeply respected and could learn a lot from. I asked John if he would be willing to meet with me periodically as a mentor and friend. How fitting that the first book John and I would read together would be Henry Scougal's, *The Life of God in the Soul of Man*; a letter written from one friend to another, in response to a request to be mentored. Our friendship deepened in Kansas City over the years that followed. There are few men whom I love deeper or respect more than my dear friend, John Gillespie. *The Life of God in the Soul of Man* was written as a letter, one man to another. If possible, I recommend that you read John's interpretation of Henry Scougal's classic as it was meant to be read... In fellowship with another brother in Christ.

John continues to travel to Haiti twice per year to train GO Project pastor partners in addition to travelling globally to train pastors through his ministry with Global Training Network. He graciously remains my good friend and mentor. We should all be so lucky.

I am happy to commend this little volume to you, confident that it will do your soul a great deal of good.

Welcome to True Life

~⁀

SOME YEARS AGO, MY FRIEND and Gospel hero, Julian Rebera, pointed me to a little book written a long time ago by a man who died before he lived out his twenty-eighth year. Over the years I have read and re-read that little book, often in the company of one or two others, to the good of our souls.

Henry Scougal was born in Scotland in 1650. He died in 1678. By the ripe old age of nineteen he was professor of Philosophy at Aberdeen University.

Being asked by a friend to disciple him in the Christian Life, Scougal wrote him a long letter explaining what it meant to be a true Christian. He never intended for that letter to become a book, only granting permission for its publication shortly before his young death. That work, *The Life of God in the Soul of Man*, was destined to become a life-changing book for countless lives.

A century after its publication, Charles Wesley gave a copy of the book to his young friend George Whitefield. Whitefield read it, saying that he never really understood True Christianity until he read Scougal's book. The rest, as we say, is history, as Whitefield went on to be the premier preacher of his day on both sides of the Atlantic and the voice behind the Great Awakening of the Eighteenth Century.

Scougal's book has fallen out of fashion in our day. How could it not? It is deep in a shallow age, serious in a trivial age, Heaven-bound in an earth-bound age. It is written to stir the heart and deliver the reader from foolish living. *The Life of God in the Soul of Man* was not, and is not, "cool" (Is not "cool" just another word for "lukewarm"?) It is simple and serious. I have made no attempt to make it cool. That would spoil its impact and be unfaithful to Henry's heart. It presents Christianity as nothing less than a supernatural, heavenly *union* of God's Life with ours. Its grand thesis is summed up in the soul-shaping truth: *The health and well-being of your soul is determined and measured by the value of that which you love the most.* It therefore relentlessly points us Godward.

So, having myself been touched many times by its fire, I have attempted to present a new interpretation of this powerful little book. I say *interpretation* for that is what this is. I have made Scougal's thoughts my own, and therefore this little book is my interpretation and explanation of his, not just his words modernized. So, if at some point you do not like it, blame me not Henry! My hope that perhaps my offering can do for many today what Scougal's did for many in past days.

A few things have guided me in the writing of this interpretation. First, Scougal did not waste words. He was a dying man with no time to lose! Hence he comes right out at the bell throwing his punches. His work is little embellished, and I have tried to be true to his style. We are used to endless illustrations and anecdotes.

Scougal used few, so I have used few. As his work is almost all meat and little garnish, so is this interpretation.

I have been as careful as I can be to remain theologically true to Scougal. While this interpretation is my work, I have tried to remain faithful to his original intention and movement, following his melody, not coming up with my own. I have added an emphasis: I think Scougal did not speak as clearly about the wonders of the Atonement as we might hope. Perhaps this was because he lived in a more Gospel-literate age when the Cross, in all its power, was more widely known, assumed, and rejoiced in. Whatever the case, I have attempted to speak more readily of the atoning work of Jesus. There have also been more than a few instances where I have expanded Scougal's original, not in theology or intent, but in adding an observation, application, or challenge which I have felt will be helpful to you, and needful in our pleasure-crazed and ease-addicted culture. In that sense, this is no longer Scougal's letter to his friend, but my letter to you.

I have also replaced his reference to "religion" with the words "True Life." Whatever good the term "religion" communicated in his day, it has become almost a dirty word in ours. So, his work, which describes "true religion" is here a work which describes "True Life" - by which I simply mean genuine Christianity.

Finally, I have added more Bible passages than Scougal first included. I think his letter was a bit "thin" here. Not that it was in any way unbiblical (!) but that its impact can be yet more powerful with the addition of more Scripture proofs of his arguments. The addition of these passages has turned a short book into a bit of a longer book! Nevertheless, take time with these passages. Linger over them and consider them until there you see something of the goodness and glory of God. They will do you more good than my words ever can!

I have been greatly helped by reading Scougal's original with another brother or a small group ... sentence by sentence, page by page. It has been a useful discipling tool in my ministry, just as Henry first intended it to be in his. I would suggest you do the same with this interpretation. Take *time* over it with a friend, perhaps an eager enquirer, a hungry new believer, or even one who has traveled long with Jesus but whose soul needs refreshment. Don't hurry! There are no rewards for reading quickly what should be read slowly! And remember: This was a *letter* before it was a *book*. Letters are more personal than books. Read this as a letter.

I have kept Scougal's three divisions, but adding titles to them which Henry did not give:

> *Part One: What is True Life?*
> *Part Two: The Wonders and Blessings of True Life*
> *Part Three: True Life is Possible!*

Be warned! Scougal will leave you without an excuse. You and I are as holy – and therefore as happy – as we want to be. True Life is not complicated, but it is challenging. It is simple, but not always easy. This book is calculated to get us to a place of desperation ... that precious soul-place where we realize that Jesus is our only Hope, and where all lesser loves bow before Him ... taking their rightful places. When there, we are on the brink of Life, the front porch of the Father's House, the suburbs of Heaven. If we miss out on True

Life, it is because we wanted less, not more, being too easily satisfied with husks; treasuring lesser gods above the only True God.

This book is not for the casual. It is for the earnest. It is my hope and prayer that it will find a home not only on your shelf, but in your heart.

Yours,

John Gillespie, Overland Park, Kansas

Christ in you, the hope of glory.

Colossians 1:27

PART ONE

What Is True Life?

~⁀

WHY I HAVE WRITTEN THIS LETTER TO YOU

My Dear Friend,

I am so glad that you have asked me to help you in your desire to follow Jesus. The direction of your heart and its aim towards God is so in step with mine, that I will find time spent with you to be a perfect use of my brief days. I believe that the most important thing is your walk with God. Therefore, I could not be a better friend to you than to invest in your holiness and growth as a Christian.

I cannot think of a better way to show my love for you and to express my thankfulness to you for being my brother, than to waste no time in getting on with this! While I am sure you could find someone better to disciple you, and I probably won't say much that you do not already know, still I hope that in God's hands, and by God's guidance, what I have to share with you will be of use to your life and soul. What an honour this is for me!

NOT THE EASY OPTION!

I NEED TO TELL YOU from the start that following Jesus is not the easy option for your life! In fact, I can tell you straight out that if you want an easy life, stay away from Jesus! There is no "fine print." Jesus tells us from the start: "Whoever wants to be my disciple must deny themselves and take up their cross daily and follow me." (Luke 9:23). It is not an easy life being offered, but True Life. As long as you understand this from the start, then all will be well. But, if anyone starts down this road mistakenly thinking that it is a flower-strewn pathway to a playground, rather than a rugged and narrow road that leads to a battlefield, they will soon be discouraged and disappointed with the Jesus they have invented in their own thoughts.

But take courage! God is ready and willing and your reward will be nothing less than Christ Himself. You will find the very Life of God residing in your soul:

> That Christ may dwell in your hearts by faith.
> (Ephesians 3:17)

You have begun a quest for True Life, and you will not be denied, so long as you are willing and ready to give all for it.

> The kingdom of heaven is like treasure hidden in a field. When a man found it, he hid it again, and then in his joy went and sold all he had and bought that field. Again, the kingdom of heaven is like a merchant looking for fine pearls. When he found one of great value, he went away and sold everything he had and bought it. (Matthew 13:44-46)

> I have come that they may have life, and
> have it to the full. (John 10:10)

FOUR THINGS BEFORE WE GO FURTHER
1) GOD IS A WILLING GOD

You must be sure of God's heart in this. He is not hiding. He is not difficult. He is not begrudging His goodness. He desires *us* more than we desire *Him*. You will therefore find a willing God and an open Heaven in your desire for True Life. This is what God really is like.

This is the entire theme of the Bible: A Redeeming God who desires and secures for Himself a redeemed people. Being sure of *His* heart for *you* from the start will encourage *your* heart for *Him*.

> For everyone who asks receives; the one who seeks finds; and to the one who knocks, the door will be opened. Which of you fathers, if your son asks for a fish, will give him a snake instead? Or if he asks for an egg, will give him a scorpion? If you then, though you are evil, know how to give good gifts to your children, how much more will your Father in heaven give the Holy Spirit to those who ask him! (Luke 11:10-13)

> I belong to my beloved and his desire is for me.
> (Song of Solomon 7:10)

2) BE SURE YOU ARE A CHRISTIAN!

I do not want to assume anything here. I am daring to remind you of the way into the Christian Life. There is only one way in, and that is through trusting in what Jesus Christ accomplished on the Cross for you. It was there that your sins were paid for in full. A Christian is one who has placed all his hope and trust in what Jesus has done, and no confidence in what he himself might hope to do – in a "religious" sense – to appease God.

If you are truly a Christian, then it is always a refreshment to your soul to hear about Jesus bearing your sins. If you are not a Christian, then it is an irritant because it grates against your pride. So, check yourself here before we proceed! Here is the acid test: How you respond to being reminded that Jesus has paid for your sins? How do you react to being told that there is no way into Life other than through simple reliance upon His amazing, sufficient death for your sins? Do you glory in it or groan against it?

> May I never boast except in the cross of our Lord Jesus Christ, through which the world has been crucified to me, and I to the world. (Galatians 6:14)

> God made him who had no sin to be sin for us, so that in him we might become the righteousness of God. (2 Corinthians 5:21)

But my friend! Do not confuse "simple" faith with something light and easy. By "simple" I mean faith in Jesus and *nothing else*. And, as such, there is nothing more radical in all the world. Simple faith in Jesus means you have renounced your own righteousness, and every other "way" to God as false and empty. It will pit you against your lazy and indifferent culture, and will cost you everything – but its reward will be Life!

3) *ARE YOU DESPERATE?*

I am assuming that in asking me to disciple you that there is a desperation in your life for Jesus Christ. It cannot be any other way. Jesus cannot just be an addition to your already happy life to make it a bit better (like a hobby or pastime). I trust you have come to the "point of no return" where you see that it is Jesus or nothing. That is the best place you can possibly be! Those who want Jesus "and" … " or Jesus "with" … end up getting the "and" or the "with" … but not getting Jesus. You need to be in the place that Peter and friends were: "Lord, to whom shall we go? You have the words of eternal life." (John 6:68). I trust that you are in that good place!

Should you dare to pray "Turn my heart towards your statutes and not towards selfish gain." (Psalm 119:36), know that those three words, "Turn my heart" imply absolute surrender of all that you are to all that God is and all that He has for you. You are saying: "Lord, I really trust your goodness towards me, and I want to loveYou more than sex or money or comfort or marriage or life itself." There is no bargaining with God. It is Life on His terms, or death on yours. Everything is at stake. While there is no place here for the half-hearted, be assured there is an open-hearted God and boundless space for the desperate!

4) DON'T TRY TO DO THIS BY YOURSELF

My friend, everything that follows in the rest of this letter assumes that you are walking with other Christians – other brothers and sisters who also want to follow Jesus. The blessings and the battles of the Christian Life are not experienced in solitude, but in the fellowship of believers. The Christian life is *personal* but not *private.* It is as you walk with others, come under the authority of the Bible preached with others, and are accountable to others that balance and genuine growth will be assured. If you separate from others, it is a sure sign of spiritual pride and you are certain to make a shipwreck of your quest for True Life.

The Bible assumes everywhere that believers are in union with each other, even as they are with Christ. There is no picture in the

New Testament of the solitary Christian who does not need other believers. It is within the context of *being together* in Jesus' Church that we truly know Jesus. True Life is not *just* "Jesus and me," it is also "Jesus and my brothers and sisters!" for we are a body together.

> Now you are the body of Christ, and each one of you is a part of it. (1 Corinthians 12:27)

> But if we walk in the light, as he is in the light, we have fellowship with one another, and the blood of Jesus, his Son, purifies us from all sin. (1 John 1:7)

> And let us consider how we may spur one another on towards love and good deeds, not giving up meeting together, as some are in the habit of doing, but encouraging one another – and all the more as you see the Day approaching. (Hebrews 10:24,25)

IF YOU ARE SURE YOU STILL WANT TO LEARN THE WAY OF TRUE LIFE IN JESUS, THEN, LET'S BEGIN!

Please forgive me for beginning with the basics. I realize you might know these things, but even so, I think it is important to lay a good foundation. It never hurts to revisit vital truths.

The Christian Life is a supernatural life. It is not just some ideas about God, or a set of rules, or a new effort to live a better life. It is a life of faith. It is a life where the wonders of Jesus Christ - who He is, and what He does, has done, and will do – grips us. It is a life lived in the wonder of the Gospel. It is a life lived by the power of the undeserved goodness of God. It is a life lived in the reality of a past forgiven and a future secure. It is a life indwelt by the Holy Spirit of God Himself – a supernatural *union* of a forgiven sinner with a gracious Saviour.

It is True Life.

But it has become so misunderstood, so complicated, so misrepresented! The simplicity that is Jesus and His Gospel has become a "religion" – human efforts to appease God. The crystal stream of the Christian life often becomes a stagnant puddle. Yet God wants for you, and me, and every simple believer nothing less than Himself living within, and True Life coming from deep in our hearts. Jesus said:

> "Let anyone who is thirsty come to me and drink. Whoever believes in me, as Scripture has said, rivers of living water will flow from within them." By this he meant the Spirit, whom those who believed in him were later to receive. (John 7:37-39)

So, I am afraid I have to start with some negatives. That really is not the direction of my heart ... pointing out problems gives me no joy ... but I need to do this.

COMMON MISTAKES

Perhaps the most common mistake in understanding True Life is simply confusing right belief – orthodox ideas – with true spiritual life. It may not be kind to refer to people as "pretenders," but that is what we are if we simply define ourselves by our attachment to a certain church or persuasion and think that this makes us true followers of Jesus. No wonder Christianity is divided into endless groups when so many think that their identity to their little sect is what makes them real Christians. Yes right belief is vital. True Life cannot spring from what is false. But being able to pass a theology exam (even earning a degree in theology!) does not guarantee the Life of God residing in the soul. The Bible tells us that even the demons believe (James 2:19). Presumably they could pass a theology exam, but certainly do not have the Life of God within!

Still others place their confidence in the doing of their duties, as if this makes them true Christians. Duties are good, but they are to spring *from* True Life, not be a substitute for it. Being kind to others, faithful at church, giving to the poor, keeping up your personal "quiet time" are all good things, but if one thinks that in keeping these he is thereby experiencing what Jesus has for him, then he is sadly mistaken. We do not *do* Christian things in order to *become* Christians. First, we become new in Jesus and then we live out our new lives. Just as a man becomes a soldier before he lives like a soldier, becoming always goes before doing.

Then there are those of us who place confidence in our feelings and experiences. It is actually easy to fool yourself here! Of course we want to truly engage our hearts with God, but if we mistake our zeal and passions with True Life, then we are misplacing our confidence. Some think that the most important thing is how we feel - as though our affection makes up for any and every other flaw. But even loud or emotional prayer, and addressing Jesus with expressions of love and passion – again, all good in their right place – do not in themselves make someone a partaker of True Life.

We are so capable of self-deception. We can mistake our sweat and loud voices for true heart life! Or, we can think our morose pride is Christian sobriety. Our anger towards others we can mistake as true zeal for the cause of Christ. Our bad attitudes toward our bosses or parents or leaders we can see as bravery and resolve. Hence, how important it is that we come to truly understand the True Life that Jesus longs to impart to us!

That is what this letter is about!

THE MIRACLE OF TRUE LIFE

Let me begin by describing True Life to you. I am not going to fall prey to the temptation just to "tell you what to do." That is all too common a mistake! "Being" is before "doing." Let's start by exploring genuine Christian experience, and talk about doing later.

True Life is a very different thing from the mere shadowy imitations we so often see around us. Those who have begun to experience what the Lord has for them have no time and no love for the false. A Christian is beginning to know, not just by his creed, but actually in his experience, that True Life is nothing less than *the union of his life with God* ... God's very life being implanted within his, or as the Apostle Paul put it, Christ being formed within us (*c.f.* Galatians 4:19). We are talking about God the Holy Spirit actually living within the believer!

> Don't you know that you yourselves are God's temple and that God's Spirit lives among you? (1 Corinthians 3:16)

So, Christianity, True Life, is nothing less, and nothing more, than the Life of God in the Soul of Man; God the Holy Spirit indwelling the believer. While it embraces creed and feelings, duties and doctrines, it goes beyond: It is a *Divine Life*. It is *supernatural*.

I want to present this Divine Life to you first by seeing how it is a *Life* and then how it is a *Divine Life*.

THE TRUE LIFE THAT CHRIST GIVES IS PERMANENT AND STABLE

First, I am choosing to call Christianity *Life. Life* speaks of something that lasts and can be counted upon, as opposed to something that is fleeting or momentary. It implies growth and vitality. True Life is not just a sudden happening, or passing emotion - even one that seemingly transports to a spiritual ecstasy. It is not at all unusual for many to have seasons of incredible "religious" activity, feeling, or seemingly unexplainable experiences. Some seem to grow at an astonishing rate, but then suddenly wither away. They start hot, but sooner or later they grow cool.

> That same day Jesus went out of the house and sat by the lake. Such large crowds gathered round him that he got into a boat and sat in it, while all the people stood on the shore. Then he told them many things in parables, saying: 'A farmer went out to sow his seed. As he was scattering the seed, some fell along the path, and the birds came and ate it up. Some fell on rocky places, where it did not have much soil. It sprang up quickly, because the soil was shallow. But when the sun came up, the plants were scorched, and they withered because they had no root … Whoever has ears, let them hear.' (Matthew 13:1-8)

Whatever has happened has not been a true work of God bringing True Life to the soul. Like bodies suddenly beheaded, they have plenty of movement, but the life is gone … however profound the agitation, there is no way it can last. In contrast, the way of a true Christian, in whom dwells True Life, will prove steady and constant and enduring because it proceeds from a union with Divine Life itself.

TRUE LIFE IS FREE AND NOT COMPELLED BY EXTERNAL FORCE, BUT INTERNAL LIFE

The simple genuine believer in Jesus is the possessor of True Life. He is not compelled by threats. He is not lured by promises of wealth or health. He is not a legalist who is simply obeying outward rules. Within him dwells the free, unbounded, love of God – Life itself. So, he is not outwardly compelled, but inwardly moved and empowered. *God has put His very Life into him.*

> For this reason I kneel before the Father, from whom every family in heaven and on earth derives its name. I pray that out of his glorious riches he may strengthen you with power through his Spirit in your inner being, so that Christ may dwell in your hearts through faith. And I pray that you, being rooted and established in love, may have power, together with all the Lord's holy people, to grasp how wide and long and high and deep is the love of Christ, and to know this love that surpasses knowledge – that you may be filled to the measure of all the fullness of God. (Ephesians 3:14-19)

So, the love which an earnest believer has towards both God and the good things of God (as opposed to the sinful things he used to love) is not the result of outward pressure, or rules, or commands, but springs from something within, which God has put there ... a new nature! Likewise, even in his secret life, a possessor of True Life does not read his Bible and pray because of obligation. He is not trying to keep God happy, or to quiet his conscience, but his devotion springs from the Divine Life that is in him. It is now the "natural" (*super*naturally caused) thing to do because he has been born again ... his soul has come to life. His prayer life, his diligence to repent, and his desire to be with God do not merely arise from duty, but from both a deep desire and a deep sense of his need for the Lord.

Therefore, if anyone is in Christ, the new creation has come: the old has gone, the new is here! (2 Corinthians 5:17)

So, he prays, and reads his Bible, and repents not because he is forced, but because he is aware of how desperate he is for God, how good and gracious God is to him, and how foolish it is to live without the Lord and to follow the path of sin … which leads only to misery. He has been re-wired, re-oriented, changed. He lives in wonder and amazement that Christ has taken his sin upon Himself on the Cross (2 Corinthians 5:21) and never forgets the glorious fact that his sins have been carried away (*c.f.* John 1:29).

But thanks be to God that, though you used to be slaves to sin, you have come to obey from your heart the pattern of teaching that has now claimed your allegiance. You have been set free from sin and have become slaves to righteousness. (Romans 6:17,18)

Likewise, the good he does - acts of charity and kindness are not forced by legalism without, but spring from love within. While no obligation is forced upon him, nevertheless his heart cannot help but be moved to charity and openness to others. To live unjustly towards others, or wildly and foolishly are now contrary to his new nature. This is all supernatural. Hence, John can (dare to) say: "No one who is born of God will continue to sin, because God's seed re-mains in them; they cannot go on sinning, because they have been born of God." (1 John 3:9). Sure, the Christian has an eye for God's Law, and honours it, but he obeys God's law not because he is afraid of its sanctions, but because he actually sees its goodness and purity. This is a revolution in the way he sees things. Again, he is moved not from outward pressure, but from inward love. He plainly sees that God's law is good and reasonable, and that there is for him great reward in obedience. God's law, once resented, is now loved and kept with new-found power.

> The law of the Lord is perfect,
> refreshing the soul.
> The statutes of the Lord are trustworthy,
> making wise the simple.
> The precepts of the Lord are right,
> giving joy to the heart.
> The commands of the Lord are radiant,
> giving light to the eyes.
> The fear of the Lord is pure,
> enduring for ever.
> The decrees of the Lord are firm,
> and all of them are righteous.
> They are more precious than gold,
> than much pure gold;
> they are sweeter than honey,
> than honey from the honeycomb.
> By them your servant is warned;
> in keeping them there is great reward.
> (Psalm 19: 7-11)

Those who are filled with the love of God normally need not be motivated by threats and rules. Love is a more powerful mover than law.

Think about Jesus. What did He say motivated Him? Outward pressure from His Father? A rule book? Remember what He said when His (shocked) disciples found Him spending time with the Samaritan woman? " My food," said Jesus, "is to do the will of him who sent me and to finish his work." (John 4:34). Just like we are hungry for food, and satisfied by it, so a believer is "naturally" (really, it is *super*natural, because God has put a new nature in him) drawn toward the will of God and is only satisfied by doing it. He is not forced to it; he is happily drawn to it. I am not saying that outward pressure is never necessary, but it is not the usual way for a true believer who possesses True Life. Maybe a baby Christian – or a faltering, worldly one - needs chiding and to be pushed along or moved to action by hopes or fears or the pressure of others, but this is not the normal case for the Christian.

Here is some good news for you: If you are seeking to be faithful and earnest in your walk with God, if you are desiring to be happy and obedient in doing God's will, if you are hoping for True Life to spring from within you, rather than being compelled by things outside of you, then take heart! These are sure signs of True Life growing within you, even if it be just a small and tender shoot. Be sure that God in Heaven will cherish the smallest evidence of His Life within you and will ensure its progress and growth.

> … being confident of this, that he who began a good work in you will carry it on to completion until the day of Christ Jesus. (Philippians 1:6)

> A bruised reed he will not break, and a smouldering wick he will not snuff out. (Matthew 12:20)

But – take warning – he who finds no such life stirring inside (even in the smallest form), and doesn't even desire it, but is happy and perfectly content with a life shaped by custom, crowd following, or outward religion ... can no more be called a true Christian than a puppet can be called a person.

Religion - by that I mean, the formal, forced, rule-based attempts to appease God, others, and one's own conscience - produces a heaviness of spirit. It is likened to pushing a heavy weight uphill. It is like a wife ever seeking to do her duty – perhaps saving face - in a loveless marriage. You can see plainly that such religion cannot produce a free and generous heart. It is like a corpse: cold and lifeless. It has the form of godliness, but none of its power (*c.f.* 2 Timothy 3:5). It will always be stingy in giving –exactly the opposite of what the Lord is like and what His grace produces in a simple believer. If True Life is the product of super-abundant grace, and therefore produces super-abundant living and giving, then legalism, the product of works-based religion, can only produce cold, calculated living which always does just what is required and no more.

> Out of his fullness we have all received grace in place of grace already given. For the law was given through Moses; grace and truth came through Jesus Christ. (John 1:16,17)

Far from being cold and calculating, the person who has given himself wholly to Jesus will never think that he is doing too much for Him. The word sacrifice, in reference to himself and his works, will not even be a part of his vocabulary.

TRUE LIFE IS A DIVINE, SUPERNATURAL LIFE

I hope it is plain to you now that Christianity – True Life – is totally different from mere forced obedience to outward religious pressure. It is a living principle within one's heart, birthed there by God Himself. It is not and cannot be sustained or motivated by weak external things like hope of reward or fear of punishment, even if such things really do exist and are true. They are but secondary motivations and empowerments for the Christian.

Having established that we are dealing here with Life and not just going through the motions of life (like a headless chicken), we need to see that this Life is a *Divine* Life. That is, it comes from God and is totally dependent upon Him. God is the fountain and source, and the sustainer of True Life: "In Him was Life …" (John 1:4). Through His Holy Spirit He implants Life into those who otherwise would have only physical life. It is also a Divine Life because it bears a resemblance to the very nature of God when it is birthed in the heart of a sinner. It is like a beam of divine light shining into – and out of – an otherwise sin-darkened life, or a drop of God's infinite ocean of goodness being placed into the heart of a believer. It is the Image of God being restored and shining in the soul of a redeemed person. That is what the Bible means when it refers to Christians as being born again, indwelt by God, or Christ being formed within them.

When the very religious Nicodemus ventured to ask Jesus about the Kingdom of God (John 3), Jesus explained to the bewildered leader that something had to happen to him if he was to enter God's Kingdom (experience True Life). When Jesus says to Nicodemus "You must be born again," (John 3:6), Jesus is not shaking His finger at the man and ordering *him* to "do" something, but He is explaining what *God* wants to do in him – impart His New Life into Nicodemus.

'This is the covenant I will make with them
after that time,' says the Lord.
'I will put my laws in their hearts,
and I will write them on their minds.'
(Hebrews 10:16)

I will give you a new heart and put a new spirit in you;
I will remove from you your heart of stone
and give you a heart of flesh.
And I will put my Spirit in you and move you to fol-
low my decrees and be careful to keep my laws.
(Ezekiel 36:26-27)

IF CHRISTIANITY IS A SUPERNATURAL LIFE, THEN WHAT IS NATURAL LIFE?

Let's go further with this. I want to make sure you see the vital difference between mere physical or "animal" life and what God wants to
impart to you. So, before we explore true spiritual life – supernatural
life – it will help if we understand natural or "animal" life. By understanding the lesser we will better understand the greater. Natural
life is what everyone has by virtue of physical birth. It is character-
ized by our desire for what is pleasing to ourselves, to our nature. It
fuels selfishness and self-love, and it spreads wildly throughout not
only each person, but throughout cultures and societies. Such natural (animal) life is founded in our feelings and senses: what we can
touch, taste, see, smell, feel, and hear, whereas supernatural life is
founded not only upon what we can sense, but also upon faith. The
most important thing to understand is that whole aim of the natural
life is to bring pleasure to the self-life.

In and of itself our natural life is not evil. It has been given
by the wisdom and goodness of God. At their best, our natural
desires and appetites drive us to preserve our lives, to take care of
ourselves, and those around us. Even simple beasts are motivated
by desires to preserve themselves and their kind. But *humans*, made
in God's image, are created for more than just natural life and animal desires. We are to be guided by something higher than simple

preservation and betterment of our physical lives. Therefore it is a crime against God - and His image that we bear - when we get all caught up in and thrilled by the things of our natural lives (as if we are *only* animals – even "higher" ones) to the neglect of our more noble purpose and our higher design. I am not in any way suggesting that our natural life is to be destroyed (it is a creation of God), but that it is to be *ruled*, *tethered*, and *governed* by our super-natural, Spiritual Life. The lower is to serve the higher. The main difference between a once-born person and a twice-born person is very simply this: The natural impulses rule the natural man, and the Divine impulses rule the supernatural man. We need to understand that to settle for the natural when we are called to the supernatural, to simply revel in the animal to the neglect of the spiritual, is true wickedness.

SOME TRADEMARKS OF THE NATURAL LIFE

The natural life is dangerously deceptive. It can carry people away into actions and habits, some of which are obviously horrible, others polite and acceptable, all depending upon the circumstances which are pressing upon it. A given person may see his actions as compara-tively good and right (and therefore think very well of himself) not realizing that they in fact spring from the same source as outwardly wicked behavior.

Think about this with me. Just consider how some people are naturally. Some are light-hearted, perhaps even to the point of fool-ishness and ridiculous behavior. Others might be serious and always composed, not daring to behave in foolish and extravagant ways. So, people see them as comparatively good and reverent and the others as bad. People esteem the one and shun the other. But is that how God sees things? …

Still others seem to be born miserable. There they are: morose and sour. They shun company and seem to spread misery wherever they go. Thankfully, everyone is not like them! Then there are others who seem to have such a sweet nature. You just want to be around them, and they love to be around others. They are naturally pleasant, considerate of others, and spread cheer wherever they go. The world seems to be a better place because of them! It is all too easy to see the former as evil and the latter as righteous. But what does God see? ...

Some have never had natural advantages of being taught how to behave towards others. They just follow their animal instincts to seek out their greatest pleasure and to work all things to their own advantage. Others have been taught right behavior and decency. They would not think of doing the base and indecent things that others do. They seem to be incapable of bad behavior. Does this mean they are better before God than the ignorant? ...

A person can actually reason himself out of bad behavior towards good behavior ... and still be not in any way a Christian. He can reason that drunkenness and lust and all other types of destructive behavior are ruining him and his reputation and muster up his natural powers to reform himself. This can be the power of nothing greater than self-love. Everyone may see him as a righteous man, when in fact he is motivated by nothing greater than pride, or reputation, or love of his money (which he realized his bad behavior was wasting). He sees that the best way to secure his personal interest in the world is to behave himself.

But the natural self can be even more self-deceived. A completely natural person might even become very "religious" and journey far on the high road of self-righteousness, learning, and piety. One might study theology, adding such impressive knowledge to his already impressive life. Others might become amazed and love to be in the company of one so learned and pious. He or she might even teach, preach, and expound knowledge of the Bible and theology all to the service of self-life. Think of how *religious* the Apostle Paul was *before* he was a Christian:

> If someone else thinks they have reasons to put confidence in the flesh, I have more: circumcised on the eighth day, of the people of Israel, of the tribe of Benjamin, a Hebrew of Hebrews; in regard to the law, a Pharisee; as for zeal, persecuting the church; as for righteousness based on the law, faultless.
>
> But whatever were gains to me I now consider loss for the sake of Christ. What is more, I consider everything a loss because of the surpassing worth of knowing Christ Jesus my Lord, for whose sake I have lost all things. I consider them garbage, that I may gain Christ and be found in him, not having a righteousness of my own that comes from the law, but that which is through faith in Christ – the righteousness that comes from God on the basis of faith. (Philippians 3:3-9)

Likewise, Jesus told a story about a man who was very religious, but not right before God:

> To some who were confident of their own righteousness and looked down on everyone else, Jesus told this parable: 'Two men went up to the temple to pray, one a Pharisee and the other a tax collector. The Pharisee stood by himself and prayed: "God, I thank you that I am not like other people – robbers, evildoers, adulterers – or even like this tax collector. I fast twice a week and give a tenth of all I get."

But the tax collector stood at a distance. He would not even look up to heaven, but beat his breast and said, "God, have mercy on me, a sinner." I tell you that this man, rather than the other, went home justified before God. For all those who exalt themselves will be humbled, and those who humble themselves will be exalted. (Luke 18:9-14)

A life collapsed in upon itself in self-love can even desire to hear of, think of, and speak of Heaven. And why not? The Bible speaks so wonderfully of Heaven: Word pictures of crowns and crystal rivers and eternal pleasures can make any worldly person want to be there – ignoring the fact that the central joy of Heaven is the very presence of our wonderful God. Even so, when a lover of self hears that Jesus has made Heaven possible, purchasing people for it with His own blood, he might even find a tender affection for Jesus, an appreciation of Him in his feelings: "How wonderful Jesus is!" Therefore he may think that he loves Jesus, when in fact he does not love the Jesus that the Bible talks about: The King of Kings and the Lord of Lords. He simply loves a Jesus he has shaped in his own mind who will serve his base, selfish purposes. Artists, musicians, poets, all sorts of people can speak and sing warmly of Jesus without bowing before Him as Lord. It is all "natural" and not necessarily supernatural at all.

So, to sum this up, I am not saying that it is evil for people to use their natural advantages to better themselves, or to encourage themselves to act in a decent manner. But, if we get carried away with the mere natural, and mistake it for the supernatural ("life" for Life) then we have stepped out of bounds and have made a serious mistake in judgment. What a person is naturally – educated or simple, polite or coarse, religious or secular – does not necessarily say anything about the deeper state of his heart.

WHAT THE SUPERNATURAL LIFE IS LIKE: FAITH FOCUSED ON FOUR ESSENTIALS

It is time now to pick up again our discovery of the supernatural life, or True Life. I am going to describe it first, and then I will offer help in experiencing it for yourself. So, don't despair when you see how wonderful it is! It is not impossible!

Remember, it is a *union* of a life with God Himself. It can be summed up in the Bible's description: "A life hidden with Christ in God."

> For you died, and your life is now hid-
> den with Christ in God.
> (Colossians 3:3)

> God has chosen to make known among the Gentiles
> the glorious riches of this mystery, which is Christ
> in you, the hope of glory. (Colossians 1:27)

> I have been crucified with Christ and I no lon-
> ger live, but Christ lives in me. The life I now
> live in the body, I live by faith in the Son of God,
> who loved me and gave himself for me.
> (Galatians 2:20)

Because it is a life "hidden with Christ," it is therefore not about display. The world around is not necessarily impressed with the supernatural life of the Christian, and it is vain for the Christian to try to impress the world with his spirituality or spiritual power. The unbeliever – who possesses nothing more than animal life – is usually unimpressed with True Life when he sees it, may not even recognize it, and if he does, will think it worthless and silly. Natural life is surrounded by self, loves itself and terminates in itself. It is narrow and occupies a very small sphere. Its highest goal is to please its lower nature. It is therefore continually attracted towards those things that will please and serve that nature.

On the contrary, True Life has lifted its sights to the limitless love of God, and has claimed lordship over its lower nature. As long as it is controlling one's life, it will never give one over to the urges and insistence of the lower life.

True Life's root is faith ... not just a vague belief, but a very focused, specific faith in Jesus Christ and His Gospel. The Apostle Paul very succinctly defines the Gospel – faith's focus - for us:

For what I received I passed on to you as of first importance: that Christ died for our sins according to the Scriptures, that he was buried, that he was raised on the third day according to the Scriptures ... (1 Corninthians 15:1-4)

Gospel focused faith is expressed in four key ways: 1) True love towards God, 2) A charitable heart towards people, 3) A heart for purity, 4) Humility towards self.

We can call these four essentials the branches of True Life. As simple as this description may sound, it is actually a picture of a life so beautified by grace, that no angel or person can conceive or tell of anything more excellent or worthy of praise.

One of them, an expert in the law, tested him with this question: "Teacher, which is the greatest commandment in the Law?'

Jesus replied: "Love the Lord your God with all your heart and with all your soul and with all your mind." This is

the first and greatest commandment. And the second is like it: "Love your neighbour as yourself." All the Law and the Prophets hang on these two commandments.
(Matthew 22: 35-40)

Rather, clothe yourselves with the Lord Jesus Christ, and do not think about how to gratify the desires of the flesh. (Romans 13:14)

Faith works in the supernatural Life in the same way that senses work in the natural life. Just like sight and smell, touch and hearing enable us to engage with the natural world, so faith enables us to engage with the supernatural world. It is spiritual vision. By faith we receive Divine truths as being true, beginning with the Gospel. So, again, faith is not some nebulous, undefined feeling, but an apprehension, a conviction that God has had mercy on us through Jesus. "Faith" means "faith *in Jesus Christ*, crucified and risen."

I am sending you to them to open their eyes and turn them from darkness to light, and from the power of Satan to God, so that they may receive forgiveness of sins and a place among those who are sanctified by faith in me. (Acts 26:17,18)

I pray that the eyes of your heart may be enlightened in order that you may know the hope to which he has called you, the riches of his glorious inheritance in his holy people, and his incomparably great power for us who believe. (Ephesians 1: 18-19)

THE FOUR BRANCHES OF TRUE LIFE

I want to briefly show you the four main branches of True Life. Remember, all I am doing right now is describing True Life. We are not talking about what we do yet! We will go deeper with them a little later, but here they are in a nutshell:

1) Love toward God. When, by faith, one believes the Gospel and is awake to the fact of God's love, the soul cannot help but give itself wholly and gladly back to Him who loved it first … and proved it on a cross (*c.f.* Romans 5:6-8). Love directed toward God is the first "branch" which springs from the root of faith. True Life desires most to please the source of that Life. This is not legalism, but the inevitable result of the love of God being received by faith. Likewise, the believer in Jesus cannot help but want to be with Jesus, and really does begin to walk in a relationship with Christ, by faith. Even more, he is ready to suffer for Jesus, or to do anything to promote His fame. Whatever Jesus prompts him to do he is ready. A believer's heart of love for his God begins with understanding the love God first had for him. That love was displayed first in the Gospel. Then it grows to embrace all of God's goodness evident in every corner of God's creation, works, and word.

2) Love toward others. But True Life does not end with love toward God. It cannot. It spreads to people – His wondrous creation, bearing His Image, intimately related to Him. This love toward mankind is the second branch of the supernatural life of grace. All of our obligations towards others can simply be summed up under the heading of "Love." The follower of Jesus, born of grace, does not

stop simply at doing no harm toward his neighbor, but there is within him a growing love for all. He views a wrong done towards another as a wrong done to himself. This *is* supernatural. He has moved from the negative – disdain for others – past the neutral – ambivalence for others – to the positive – love for others.

3) Purity of heart and life. What is meant by "a heart for purity?" Christian purity begins with a mastery over self, and over the "lower" physical urges which attempt to rule one's life. There are urges and desires that are *wrong* and which will not serve the True Life which God has implanted in the child of grace. Purity is a willingness to say "no" to wicked actions and passions and "yes" to God's will. And, it goes beyond controlling one's "lower" urges and expresses itself in positive acts of courage and noble choices … that will lead to holiness and happiness.

> For the grace of God has appeared that offers salvation to all people. It teaches us to say 'No' to ungodliness and worldly passions, and to live self-controlled, upright and godly lives in this present age … (Titus 2:11,12)

4) Humility in regards to oneself. Humility is a true sense of one's own basic sinfulness, expressed in one's attitude or actions. Therefore a humble person readily and happily acknowledges that he owes all to God's overflowing, unmerited grace and bountiful goodness. It follows that a humble, thankful person will quickly and consistently submit himself to the will of God, whatever that may be, and in so doing, shun the lime-light, approval and applause of the world.

It is impossible to advance beyond these four branches. Here is Heaven being formed in the soul – right here and now. The simple follower of Jesus who is finding these profound evidences of grace in his own heart needs no further proof that he belongs to God. He does not need to discover God's secrets to know that he is born of God, for he sees the evidence right in his own heart. His love to God is evidence that he has first received God's love to him, and the beginnings of joy in wanting to do the will of God is evidence to him of a supernatural work taking place within. ... Even though it is just beginning, the fact that it has begun is evidence and proof that it will be one day completed in Heaven.

> ... being confident of this, that he who began a good work
> in you will carry it on to completion until the day of Christ
> Jesus. (Philippians 1:6)

With this in mind, you can understand why someone has said: "I would rather see the real impressions of a godlike nature upon my own soul, than have a vision from Heaven, or an angel sent to tell me that my name was written in the Book of Life."

TRUE LIFE IS BEST SEEN IN THE LIFE OF JESUS CHRIST

When we have exhausted all words, and done our best to explain the wonders of True Life, the deep mystery of what God has done and is doing in the awakened soul can never be fully explained. Experience goes beyond our ability to tell.

> My mouth will tell of your righteous deeds,
> of your saving acts all day long –
> though I know not how to relate them all. (Psalm 71:15)

There is a sense in which the work done in the depths of a Christian can only be understood by that awakened soul. It is deep. It is relational. It is personal. It is supernatural. Deep calls unto deep. The Infinite God is relating to the inner life of one made in His Image through the wonders of the Gospel and the workings of His Spirit.

There is a sense in which what is beyond explanation can better be displayed and understood by what one does more than by what one says. Remembering that all the issues of life flow from within, from the heart of a man, one's life lived is perhaps a more vivid expression of his secret life than can be otherwise known:

> Above all else, guard your heart,
> for everything you do flows from it.
> (Proverbs 4:23)

> 'No good tree bears bad fruit, nor does a bad tree bear good fruit. Each tree is recognised by its own fruit. People do not pick figs from thorn-bushes, or grapes from briers. A good man brings good things out of the good stored up in his heart, and an evil man brings evil things out of the evil stored up in his heart. For the mouth speaks what the heart is full of. (Luke 6:43-45)

Grace in the heart can best be measured by actions in the life. The best and most obvious example of this is our Lord Jesus, whose life exemplified what he taught. What He desired to see in others He lived out before them. In Him there was no contradiction between His words and His deeds. If ever True Life was lived, it was lived in Jesus. This lowly planet has actually been graced with perfection in the person and life of Jesus Christ.

The Word became flesh and made his dwelling among us. We have seen his glory, the glory of the one and only Son, who came from the Father, full of grace and truth. (John 1:14)

> As for me, I find no basis for a charge against him.' (Pilate, of Jesus. John 19:6)

We are punished justly, for we are getting what our deeds deserve. But this man has done nothing wrong. (The Dying Thief, of Jesus. Luke 23:41)

He made Him who knew no sin to be sin on our behalf, so that we might become the righteousness of God in Him. (2 Corinthians 5:21)

For we do not have a high priest who is unable to feel sympathy for our weaknesses, but we have one who has been tempted in every way, just as we are – yet he did not sin. (Hebrews 4:15)

So, let's take some time and explore these four branches of True Life in our Lord Jesus. And, be encouraged! Beholding Jesus in the Bible transforms us into His likeness:

And we all, who with unveiled faces contemplate the Lord's glory [as revealed in the Bible], are being transformed into his image with ever-increasing glory, which comes from the Lord, who is the Spirit. (2 Corinthians 3:18)

LOVE TOWARD GOD WAS TRULY SHOWN IN JESUS

Jesus Christ was filled with true love for His Father, and this was demonstrated in His continual desire to do His Father's will. His burning heart of God-ward love was happily resigned to the purposes of His Father – He actually said that doing His Father's will was his food, that is, it fed and sustained His inner life. All through Jesus' life he was engaged in doing His Father's business, even in childhood.

> He said to them, "Why were you searching for me? Did you not know that I must be in my Father's house?" But they did not understand what he said to them. (Luke 2: 49-50)

Think about His encounter in John 4 with the Samaritan woman. He went out of His way to meet her. He was happy to be hungry, weak, and weary so long as He was where His Father would have him. While His disciples went to get food, He was refreshed by His Divine appointment with that poor, broken woman.

> Meanwhile the disciples were urging him, "Rabbi, eat something." But he said to them, "I have food to eat that you do not know about." So the disciples said to one another, "Surely no one has brought him something to eat?" Jesus said to them, "My food is to do the will of him who sent me and to complete his work. (John 4:31-34)

He began His time with her with a request for water, but He finished by declaring that the doing of His Father's will had satisfied Him. It was clearly all joy for Jesus to do the will of God. Whether it would prove pleasant or difficult, Jesus was patient and diligent to do whatever His Father desired of Him.

CONSIDER HIS PATIENCE AS AN EXPRESSION OF HIS LOVE FOR HIS FATHER

It would be harder to imagine any person having to patiently endure more than Jesus. His entire life on earth was a condescension and humiliation to a degree that no one else has ever experienced:

> In your relationships with one another,
> have the same mindset as Christ Jesus:
> who, being in very nature God,
> did not consider equality with God
> something to be used to his own advantage;
> rather, he made himself nothing
> by taking the very nature - of a servant,
> being made in human likeness.
>
> And being found in appearance as a man,
> he humbled himself
> by becoming obedient to death –
> even death on a cross!
> (Philippians 2:5-8)

Yet there is no record that Jesus ever had a resentful thought or uttered a grumbling word – all the while He was fully human – not strangely fanatical, void of feeling, or stoical. He had the same range of feelings and emotions as everyone else, and probably greater, as His whole person was not affected and limited by sin. Clearly He lived in full awareness of the suffering that awaited Him on the cross (Remember, for example, when He actually sweat blood in Gethsemane as the cross loomed before Him.) Yet even then He fully submitted Himself to the will of His Father.

When in Gethsemane, Jesus prayed that if possible, if His Father willed it, the cup of God's wrath for *our* sin might pass from Him, Jesus concluded that prayer in complete submission to His Father's will: "Never the less not my will but yours be done." Even before that night, Jesus began to show us the anguish of His spirit:

> Now my soul is troubled. And what should I say—'Father, save me from this hour'? No, it is for this reason that I have come to this hour. (John 12:27)

How important were (and are) these words! They reveal so much of the heart and mind of our Lord Jesus. While they seem, at first glance, to show a hesitancy, they certainly show that Jesus really wrestled with the reality of what was before Him. His resolve is quickly established with the proclamation: "No (!), it is for this reason that I have come to this hour."

We dare not think that Jesus, in this wrestling with His Father's will in Gethsemane, was somehow blameworthy or weak. When we read the Gospel accounts it is evident throughout that Jesus always knew His purpose and destiny. He was not surprised at the cross or the redemptive will of His Father. But the Gethsemane wrestling, and the earlier words in John's Gospel do tell us of the weight – the inconceivable weight – which Jesus knew He was about to bear. There was an understandable terror to the cross. How could there not be? Yet there was a willingness, even a desire deeper than the terror, to do the will of God, knowing that His dying for sinners would glorify His Father.

PRAYER EXPRESSED JESUS' LOVE FOR HIS FATHER

Jesus' love for His Father was also demonstrated in His prayer life. Think about this: Two things which tend to drive us to prayer: 1) sins to confess and 2) earthly concerns – were absent in Jesus. Yet we find Him rising early in the morning to spend time with His Father, and staying all night in fellowship and prayer with His Father. I think we can easily deduce that it was His *pleasure* to spend time with His Father ... His entire life in a real sense was a prayer to His Father, an uninterrupted devotion and fellowship with Heaven. Like the altar in Israel's temple, even if the sacrifice was not being offered, the fire was still alive and burning. It seems that our Lord Jesus was ever careful to not be subject to that coldness of spirit that so often hinders us, which we have to overcome before we can spend time with our Heavenly Father.

> And the one who sent me is with me; he has not left me alone, for I always do what is pleasing to him. ... I knew that you always hear me, but I have said this for the sake of the crowd standing here, so that they may believe that you sent me. (John 8:29; 11:42)

> In the morning, while it was still very dark, he got up and went out to a deserted place, and there he prayed. ... Now during those days he went out to the mountain to pray; and he spent the night in prayer to God.
> (Mark 1:35; Luke 6:12)

HIS HEART OF LOVE FOR PEOPLE

If you think about it, when you read the Gospel accounts of Jesus, you can't find anything that Jesus did that was not moved by love for others and which did not somehow express that love. Jesus did not merely love His family and friends, but His love and compassion was expressed far and wide. Consider His miracles: They were not just demonstrations of His power, but also expressions of His love. Yes, they amazed those who saw them, but more, they blessed those who received them. While He had a deep love and friendship with the disciple John, He did not confine His love for people just to this deep friendship. He welcomed *all* into the warm orbit of His love and fellowship:

> Come to me, all you who are weary and burdened, and I will give you rest. Take my yoke upon you and learn from me, for I am gentle and humble in heart, and you will find rest for your souls. (Matthew 11:28-29)

> Greater love has no one than this: to lay down one's life for one's friends. You are my friends if you do what I command. (John 15:13,14)

> 'Who are my mother and my brothers?' he asked. Then he looked at those seated in a circle round him and said, 'Here are my mother and my brothers! Whoever does God's will is my brother and sister and mother.'
>   (Mark 3:33-35)

Jesus never drove anyone away. He promised His Father that He would not! *"All those the Father gives me will come to me, and whoever comes to me I will never drive away."* (John 6:35) If one came with an honest intention, Jesus received him. He was tough on the proud and the self-righteous, but readily embraced the humble and broken. The only one on record who ever came to Jesus and left sad was the rich young man (Mark 10) who didn't want to give up his idol of personal wealth to gain True Life. The Bible is careful to tell us that Jesus loved him. Even in loving him, Jesus was not going to chase after him, cut a special deal with him, and somehow make it possible for a man to keep his idols and gain True Life.

What about the proof of His love as shown in His meekness! When the treacherous traitor Judas betrayed Jesus to the soldiers, Jesus' only words to Judas were, "Do you betray me with a kiss?" He even healed the severed ear of one of His captors! Further, how more could He have proven His love, *even for His enemies*, than in laying down His life on the cross … willingly? Even as He bled, He prayed for those who crucified Him that His Father would forgive them. What love! The very blood they caused Jesus to shed was the blood that atoned for their sins!

THE PURITY OF JESUS

The third key trait of True Life is purity of heart and actions. Purity implies and involves a true desire to say "no" to the perverse enjoyments of this fallen world, and a pursuit of the pure joys of the world to come. Purity is willing to suffer here in the doing of God's will.

Jesus was dead to the sin of seeking pleasure as an end in itself. We never read of Him pursuing pleasure for pleasure's sake. Consider the joys of marriage: Jesus rejoiced to attend a wedding, enhancing it with His presence and bringing the bounty of the best wine (John 2:1-12). Yet He Himself never knew the joys of marriage or the pleasures of the marriage bed. He did not forbid it to others, but He denied it to Himself. Likewise, He could supply gallons of the best wine for others, but would not make one stone into bread for His own satisfaction. He was so full of grace that He happily supplied for others not only their greater need (salvation from sin) but also their lesser wants … even if He denied them to Himself.

While we read of Jesus' sighs, tears, and groans, there is no record of His laughter, although there is of Him being "full of joy through the Holy Spirit" (Luke 10:21). What was prophetically spoken of Him in Isaiah, that He was "a man of suffering, and familiar with pain," proved to be true (Isaiah 53:3).

Jesus, if He had wanted to, could have maintained the easiest and most comfortable life imaginable. He who could feed thousands with a few fish, find tax money in the mouth of a fish, and cause the fisherman's net to be full to break-point. He could easily have been the richest man on earth and could have raised an army and destroyed Rome in an instant. But He, whose entire life was pure in every aspect, would not do anything just to satisfy His "self." Here is One, the Creator of all things, the Owner of the Universe, who so esteemed the things we despise (humility and purity) that He had to borrow a womb for His own birth, a coin for a sermon illustration, and a tomb for His own burial! He warned the over-zealous potential follower that He had no place to lay His head.

He was not a socialite. His companions were fishermen and labourers. He kept company - not with princes and those considered to be powerful and influential – but with tax gatherers and prostitutes. His right –side-up values turned the values of the world upside-down. His social circle was a scandal to the proud of this world.

> Jesus replied, 'Go back and report to John what you hear and see: the blind receive sight, the lame walk, those who have leprosy] are cleansed, the deaf hear, the dead are raised, and the good news is proclaimed to the poor. Blessed is anyone who does not stumble on account of me.' (Matthew 11:4-6)

The son of a carpenter, He lived in such a way that befitted, not the princes, but the simple of this world. This brings us to consider the fourth branch of True Life.

THE HUMILITY OF JESUS

Jesus invites us to learn humility from Him. Imagine! The Son of God can describe Himself as "meek and lowly of heart." The King of kings is a humble servant. We could consider the infinite conde-scension of Jesus – from the wonders of Heaven to the ruins of earth (*c.f.* Philippians 2:5-11). But for now, let us consider the way in which the Lord Jesus lived while He was among us.

So often, it is sin and imperfection which humble us ... even the best of us. But Jesus, while being tempted in every way like us, never sinned. It was not sin that humbled Jesus. What humbled Jesus – the man Jesus – was a deep and abiding sense of the greatness and infinite perfection of God. In the mystery of Jesus, fully God and fully Man, the man Jesus was rightly and always aware of His small-ness before God's greatness. No doubt, those good things He found within Himself as a man He knew to be the gracious gifts of God.

How else can you explain the otherwise puzzling response Jesus gave to the young man in Mark's Gospel? Remember when the man referred to Jesus as "Good teacher?" Clearly this young man, un-aware of the fact that Jesus was both God and Man, was address-ing Jesus as to His human nature. Jesus replied in terms of His humanity: "Why do you call me good? ... No one is good – except God alone." (Mark 10:18). It was as if Jesus was saying to the young man: "Since you have addressed me as a man, I will answer you as a man. Compared to God, a man is not worthy of notice, and has no goodness in and of Himself. It is God alone who is eternally, and essentially good."

Jesus never, not once, abused His divine power for show or to promote Himself. He would not gratify others' curiosity with signs from heaven. He would not leap from the Temple to amaze peo-ple into faith. When His brothers advised Him to go to Jerusalem to go public and increase His exposure, He did not rise to their worldly-wise advice. He could have increased His presence – in a worldly way – but it was His humility that led Him to conceal His miracles. When He did go public with a miracle, His motive was that God be glorified, and He was happy to ascribe all the fame and all of the credit to His Father.

> Jesus gave them this answer: 'Very truly I tell you, the Son can do nothing by himself; he can do only what he sees his Father doing, because whatever the Father does the Son also does. (John 5:19)

> By myself I can do nothing; I judge only as I hear, and my judgment is just, for I seek not to please myself but him who sent me. (John 5:30)

> So Jesus said, 'When you have lifted up the Son of Man, then you will know that I am he and that I do nothing on my own but speak just what the Father has taught me. (John 8:28)

> Jesus replied, 'If I glorify myself, my glory means nothing. My Father, whom you claim as your God, is the one who glorifies me. (John 8:54)

The best way to get a clear understanding of true humility is to study the life of Jesus. We cannot encompass here the endless examples, but just consider the following: They came to make Him king, and he refused (John 6:15). Really think about this! How many of *us* would resist such a desire if pressed upon us by thousands of eager people? In His youth, He willingly made Himself subject to His earthly parents (Luke 2:51). Here they are: sinful; here He is: sinless, yet in obedient humility He subjugates

Himself to them. His whole life is one great record of humility. Jesus, *the Eternal Son of God* is humble before mere creatures of dust.

WE NEED TO PRAY BEFORE WE GO FURTHER

We are discovering True Life. Let's pray it into our hearts and spirits before we move on.

"Lord God! Infinite, Eternal, Majestic! Ever-flowing source of all Life and happiness! We tiny, sinful creatures of dust know so little of You and of the True Life You offer. We speak easily about Jesus and His Gospel, but how few of us actually possess True Life and understand the wonders of your ways. We so easily confuse our natural feelings and simple self-love as evidence of supernatural grace … and only Your grace – not our nature - can make us acceptable in Your sight.

It breaks our hearts when we consider how long we have walked in ignorance of You and Your ways – so far from True Life. For years we were content with the shadows, missing the substance altogether. And yet now we are so thankful and have such joy in our hearts that You in Your mercy have opened our eyes to begin to see the way of Life in Christ. You can and are changing us! You are actually imparting True Life to us, Your very nature, The Life of God within us mere humans!

Lord God! How we bless You for Your infinite mercy! That Jesus Himself has walked with us. … Your Son among us! The One who would die for our sins first showed us by His perfect life what is True Life: Love to You, Love for Others, Purity of Heart, and Humility of Character. Now Lord, form in us – even us – the very nature of Him who bore our sins. Grant us all grace that we may never cease to press in to You until Christ Himself is formed within our lowly selves."

For Your Glory and our Good. Amen!"

PART TWO

The Wonders and Blessings of True Life

∽

Understanding Will Motivate Your Pursuit

I KNOW THAT YOU ARE wanting to rush ahead, and have me tell you how to apprehend this Life. My good news for you is that the fact that you are eager is sure evidence that God has birthed this Life within you. Be patient, my dear friend. We have taken a look at the nature of True Life. Before we press on, it will be helpful to consider – feast upon – the wonders and blessings of True Life. Having done so, we will be yet more motivated to pursue that Life, and to discipline ourselves in whatever ways necessary to attain all the blessings that the Lord has designed for us.

But I have to confess right at the start, that words really cannot express the joy and fullness that True Life brings. In a real sense, only those who experience it can understand it, just as only a bride and groom can truly understand the nature of their love one for another and the particular joy it brings.

It needs to be made plain that True Life – and we can use the word *Holiness*, being set apart to know and enjoy God, here – is what we have been created for. Sin brings sickness to the soul and to the entire being. The holy soul is a healthy soul. A sin-ridden soul is sick and therefore incapable of the fullness for which it has been created. A sinful soul is weary, tossed about, and restless. When Jesus Christ brings Life through His Gospel, the disease is removed, and health is restored to the entire person. The intellect can see and understand what is good, and the will can choose and embrace it. The heart, being no longer chained to sensuality and enslaved to what can be seen and felt, is now free to be influenced by God and things of eternal value and worth. There is *total* transformation.

THE WORTH OF GOD-WARD LOVE

It is time to narrow our focus. We have looked at the main branches of True Life (love toward God, love toward others, purity, and humility). Let us now bring our attention to a deeper understanding of the most vital of all: love towards God. True Life is a union of the soul of the creature to the Life of the Creator. It is a union of love that has its origin in God and flows towards us (Creator to created), but then is returned to God, its source (created to Creator).

> This is love: not that we loved God, but that he loved us and sent his Son as an atoning sacrifice for our sins. (1 John 4:10)

> We love because He first loved us. (1 John 4:19)

There is no more powerful force in the soul than love. Our heart-affections determine the course and direction of our lives. Our happiness (or misery) is directly dependent upon the nature and object of our love. Everyone, without exception, becomes like that which he loves. Therefore: *The health and well-being of your soul is determined and measured by the value of that which you love the most.* If you love things that are dirty and impure, you yourself will become dirty and impure. But if you, with deliberate intention, place your affection on what is noble and good (and what can be more noble and good than Jesus Christ?) then your soul – the very depth of your being – will grow in health, becoming like the object of that love.

It is not surprising to find that we become like what we love most. It happens in the natural world all the time. Friends become increasingly alike as they spend time together. Husbands and wives grow remarkably alike as years pass and their affection for each other increases. They even seem to imitate one another, anticipating each other's actions, words, and even thoughts. Gestures, tone of voice, opinions take on the same shape. But since no person – even the best of us – is good to the core, and every one of us is a mixture of good and evil, then it follows that we not only take on the good of those we love, but the evil as well. When we love another, we are often and easily blind to his/her faults, so that we approve of traits we would normally shun, and soon find ourselves imitating them.

We can see here that the surest way to bring health and life to our souls is by learning to fix our affection on that which is most noble. Since there is nothing more noble and wonderful than God Himself, then clearly as we love Him above all else, our entire beings are transformed for the better.

And we all, who with unveiled faces contemplate the Lord's glory, are being transformed into his image with ever-increasing glory, which comes from the Lord, who is the Spirit. (2 Corinthians 3:18)

> Since, then, you have been raised with Christ, set your hearts on things above, where Christ is, seated at the right hand of God. Set your minds on things above, not on earthly things. For you died, and your life is now hidden with Christ in God. When Christ, who is your life, appears, then you also will appear with him in glory. (Colossians 3:1-4)

Anyone who with a sincere and earnest desire to lay hold of all for which Christ has laid hold of him, and who therefore disciplines himself to raise his thoughts and affections heaven-ward, will find a Life growing in him that the natural world cannot know. It will follow – without fail – that his affections will change. Things that used to captivate him will no longer. He will increasingly find that he does not want his old loves to displace his new, wonderful, and heavenly love.

Remember, of all our affections, feelings, and impulses, love is the greatest. There is a sense in which we can say that we are the masters of our love, for it is we who determine its object. So it follows that to give our love – our highest gift – to an unworthy object is both foolish and sinful.

We must see ourselves as in charge of our affections. (It is very tempting, but wrong, to see ourselves as at the mercy of our affections.) In a sense, our love is the only thing that we really own, and that cannot be taken from us. Once you have given your love, all other gifts follow in train. It is not possible that any lesser gift will be refused once we have given the greater gift of our love.

To love Christ supremely is to make all lesser aspects of discipleship, even those that demand suffering and loss, possible. Love is the greatest present we can offer, and God is most worthy to receive our greatest present. It follows that to give this love elsewhere, by that I mean to love anything supremely other than God, is to debase ourselves, our love, and God. Loving Christ supremely makes every lesser aspect of the Christian life possible. Loving anything else in the place of Christ makes the entire Christian life impossible.

When Jesus warns us against trying to serve two masters (Matthew 6:24), the spirit of that warning applies to vainly trying to supremely love God along with anything else. There is only room for *one* supreme love in your life.

Teacher, which is the greatest commandment in the Law? Jesus replied: "Love the Lord your God with all your heart and with all your soul and with all your mind." This is the first and greatest commandment. (Matthew 22:36-39)

No one can serve two masters. Either you will hate the one and love the other, or you will be devoted to the one and despise the other. You cannot serve both God and Money. (Matthew 6:24)

We often ascribe love to things and people which really only belongs to God. We prove with our words that we have misplaced our affection. If we think about it, and take words at face value, our own words prove that we are idolaters and blasphemers! There is a proper affection for people, but a supreme affection for God alone and we continually apply figures of speech and expressions of love to people that should belong only to God. To love something in the place of God is to do great damage to our souls. To ascribe words of love to something (even a spouse or a child) that rightly belong only to God is likewise to cause deep damage. Think for a minute of the words and expressions in so much of our music and media. Absolute supreme love is time and again ascribed to people.

Yet when God *alone* receives the supreme love of our hearts, and our words confirm that, what health that is to our souls! The chains of love with which we bind ourselves to God are in fact liberating, and to be a slave to Christ is more noble than to be the ruler of all the world.

THE BLESSINGS OF LOVING GOD ABOVE ALL ELSE

Just as love toward God brings health to the soul, so it brings ultimate joy and pleasure to the entire person. Nothing else can reach the depths and the heights of a person in the same way as responding to the love of God with love toward God. We were created for this. It is good and right to love others as an *expression* of our love for God, but dangerous to love them as a *replacement* for our love for God. Every lesser love, every idol that we adore is really just a substitute for this highest of all loves. The greatest joys, the most real, solid, and substantial delights of which we are capable, are those that grow from placing our affections where they belong: upon Jesus Christ.

What makes love turn sour is when we place it upon those who are not worthy of our ultimate love. The best humans are not worthy of your highest love. They will fail you, one way or another. They might fail to truly value the love you are giving them. They may not return your love, or they might be absent, or die, and leave you broken. Creatures cannot offer what only our Creator can. Therefore, the endless dangers and pitfalls that exist when we idolize anything – even a spouse or child – do not exist when we place our affections upon Him who alone can rightly receive them without damaging them.

THE VALUE OF THE OBJECT OF OUR LOVE

Let me begin by saying (again) that love will produce misery and tragedy when its object – due to its unworthiness and weakness - is incapable of containing it. Love is so powerful that any creature is incapable of ultimately satisfying its demands. That is why the best human love – whose ultimate object is another person, be he ever so wonderful – will be frustrated and lead to brokenness. Our love was not intended to be fully satisfied by another person, but only by God. Nothing below the infinite worth of God can afford love the room it needs to grow and thrive and exert its incredible power. We were *made for God*. Skin-deep beauty and a bit of human goodness cannot compare with the infinite goodness that God alone possesses. No wonder so many human loves end in tragedy and brokenness. How can they not? The human heart is incapable of containing, sustaining, and protecting another's heart. Jealousy, bitterness, rivalry are never far from the idolatry of misplaced love. Truly "love as strong as death" gives birth to "jealousy which is cruel as the grave." (*c.f.* Song of Solomon 8:6)

But love toward God knows nothing of this bitterness. It therefore frees the lover to truly and safely love other people. Whenever someone places his love where it belongs – in the All-Sufficient and Good God – it finds that not only is its love satisfied, but overpowered and mastered by the Love of God. There is so much "room" in God to contain our love, that the lover cannot help but see the smallness of his love. Then begins an earnest quest for an ever larger heart of love toward God. Aware of the coldness of his heart, the lover of God actually longs for the day when his heart will be inflamed with such love as only God truly deserves, and in the meantime summons others and all creation and even the angels to join with him in expressing to God the love he has for Him.

Praise the Lord, you his angels,
you mighty ones who do his bidding,
who obey his word.

Praise the Lord, all his heavenly hosts,
you his servants who do his will.
Praise the Lord, all his works
everywhere in his dominion.
Praise the Lord, my soul. (Psalm 103:20-22)

YOU CAN BE CERTAIN THAT YOUR LOVE WILL NOT BE ABUSED

Human love is vulnerable. There is no guarantee that it will be returned. Remember: You have nothing of more value to give than your love. When we give our love, we give ourselves – all that we have. Therefore, what greater pain and sorrow can we experience than when our love is under-valued and not returned? When a gift is despised, sorrow is sure to be the result and when the greatest gift is despised, the sorrow can be overwhelming.

Love is an abandoning of one's self to another. If it is true and genuine love, it is a voluntary and willing death to self. The lover despises his own interests and goals for the sake of the beloved. His whole heart is caught up in the adventure of meeting the needs and wants of the one he loves. But! If that affection is not received and returned in kind, the lover is in a real sense, destroyed by his own love. He has abandoned himself to another who cares nothing for him in return. But, if he is loved in return, then his heart is brought to life in a real sense, and the self he once abandoned for another becomes valuable again because it is valued by another.

The whole enterprise – on a purely human level – is a huge risk. The only way to safely love another person is to have your highest love placed somewhere truly safe.

But I am stating the obvious. Literature, music, media all build their stories upon the reality of fragile human love. Nothing is clearer to the entire human family than the fact that human happiness depends upon love being valued and not abused. It is just here that love toward God displays its wonder and advantage over all lesser loves. Here we are loving one who has first loved us, and who has proven and displayed that love not because we are wonderful and worthy, but while we were unworthy and wicked.

> You see, at just the right time, when we were still powerless, Christ died for the ungodly. Very rarely will anyone die for a righteous person, though for a good person someone might possibly dare to die. But God demonstrates his own love for us in this: while we were still sinners, Christ died for us. (Romans 5:6-8)

It is not possible for God to withhold His love from one who loves Him, for *He* loved *first*. Here is a heart that bears His very image, responding to His love with love: How can God reject such a heart? He cannot! A heart that desires nothing more than to love God back is a heart which He cannot and will not abuse.

> Satisfy us in the morning with your unfailing love,
> that we may sing for joy and be glad all our days.
> (Psalm 90:14)

> I have loved you with an everlasting love; I
> have drawn you with unfailing kindness.
> (Jeremiah 31:3)

You need to know that God desires your heart. He made you for Himself and He will not reject or deny your approach. As Boaz is to Ruth, so is Jesus to the poor sinner. And, as Boaz would not fail to redeem, restore, and wed the needy Ruth, so Jesus will not fail to embrace you in His covenant of love. You need to be sure of *His* heart in this matter!

> Then Naomi said, 'Wait, my daughter, until you find out what happens. For the man will not rest until the matter is settled today.' (Ruth 4:18)

GOD IS NEVER AN ABSENT LOVE

Human love will inevitably experience separation. Separation brings pain and heartbreak. This is unavoidable, even in the best human loves. Friends must part, even if for a short time. But death – inevitable death – brings a grief of separation unparalleled by all other griefs. So, separation, whether brief or permanent, is the price we pay for all human affection.

Consider the security and joy that must follow love which rests in One who will never leave or forsake us - One who, by His very nature, can never be absent. "From everlasting to everlasting the Lord's love is with those who fear Him." (Psalm 103: 17). The darkness of a prison or the loneliness of a desert cannot ablate the love of One who is ever present. The eyes of faith see their Beloved everywhere and can trace His glory in any and every situation. It is actually possible to live in uninterrupted enjoyment of the love of God.

RESPONDING TO THE LOVE OF GOD BY LOVING GOD BRINGS US INTO AN INFINITE HAPPINESS

In human love, if the beloved one is miserable, the lover is likewise miserable. When we exchange our hearts with others, their joys or miseries becomes ours. When love is earth-bound instead of Heavenly, it inevitably becomes troubled and tiresome. Think about this: The most blessed of us still has enough trouble and grief to make life a trial. And it is impossible that one's grief will not affect those who love him. When one is under attack, those who love him feel the impact as well. But, when God is the source and object of our love, there we can find a safe harbor for our hearts, and there we can find true, unassailable happiness.

> God is our refuge and strength,
> an ever-present help in trouble.
> Therefore we will not fear, though the earth give way
> and the mountains fall into the heart of the sea,
> though its waters roar and foam
> and the mountains quake with their surging.[
> There is a river whose streams make glad the city of God,
> the holy place where the Most High dwells.
> God is within her, she will not fall;
> God will help her at break of day. (Psalm 46:1-5)

God's love, and His happiness will never – in any way – diminish. In Him alone we can safely invest our love and receive all the joy and strength for which the very angels of Heaven praise Him. What a source of joy it is to consider the fact that the One we love is infinitely happy within Himself, and that all the forces of Hell cannot shake His joy for one moment!

What a sure foundation we build upon when we build upon the Lord! The one whose love is placed upon the God of happiness, whose will is being conformed to the will of the God of happiness, and whose greatest desire is to please the God of happiness, is without fail on the road to true joy. What peace, rest, and satisfaction embrace the heart and mind of the one who places his love in the God of happiness!

> The Lord delights in those who fear him,
> who put their hope in his unfailing love.
> (Psalm 147:11)

THOSE WHO LOVE GOD SUPREMELY FIND SWEETNESS IN EVERY SITUATION

I think I have said it before, but it is worth saying again: we cannot help but begin to experience infinite pleasure and joy when we become caught up in giving ourselves in holy love to our good God. When a true sense of God's goodness begins to captivate our minds and hearts and that sense is combined with a free offering of ourselves in warm affection back to God, the result must be a true and solid happiness breaking upon our souls. What a blessing it is to be weary of ourselves, and laying aside lukewarm religiosity, offer ourselves without reserve to the God who made us, gave us life, and now gives us True Life. Such an offering, when made through the atoning blood of Christ, is a holy and acceptable offering, totally pleasing to God (*c.f.* Romans 12:1-2). The lover can say without hesitation: "I am my Beloved's and His desire is for me." (Song of Songs 7:10). In such an offering is a precious liberty from self – a self-forgetfulness – that opens up a new life of radical living. The goal becomes to serve the good purposes of the lover's good God.

> You make known to me the path of life; you will fill me with joy in your presence, with eternal pleasures at your right hand. (Psalm 16:11)

Therefore, I urge you, brothers and sisters, in view of God's mercy, to offer your bodies as a living sacrifice, holy and pleasing to God – this is your true and proper worship. (Romans 12:1)

All of life is sweetened by the love of God toward us and our love to Him returned. Every situation comes under God's providential care, including the simple events of daily life. These situations both lose their significance (they cease to be idols) and take on a profound sweetness (because they have the taste of God's goodness upon them). They are messages of love sent to us by our wonderful, good Heavenly Father.

This sweetness even includes the chastisements of God, though they are not – in the moment – pleasant. The rod and staff of our Good Shepherd God may come with a sting, but they are actually accomplishing in us God's holy and wise purposes. We can rejoice when God does not agree with the will and designs of His foolish creatures but works His own will instead.

Therefore we do not lose heart. Though outwardly we are wasting away, yet inwardly we are being renewed day by day. For our light and momentary troubles are achieving for us an eternal glory that far outweighs them all. So we fix our eyes not on what is seen, but on what is unseen, since what is seen is temporary, but what is unseen is eternal. (2 Corinthians 4:16-18)

THE "DUTIES" OF THE CHRISTIAN LIFE ARE SWEET AS WELL

Some might consider the disciplines of the Christian Life to be tiresome, and foolish, but when one is responding to the God of Love with love, these disciplines bring true joy and contentment to the believer. Gathering with other believers to worship is not a dry duty but a desirous, anticipated joy (Psalm 63:2). Getting away from the fury of life to be still; to open the Bible and hear from the Lord; to silence one's noisy and restless heart and open it in prayer to the God who loves it dearly; these are sweet "duties" for the possessor of True Life. There is joy in thinking about God, in considering His ways and His character, in remembering all His goodness. It is a joy, a consummation, a completion, to proclaim one's love to God even to tell Him a thousand times that He is loved! It becomes a happy relief for the believer to unburden his troubled soul in prayer to the One who loves him, and to hand off his heavy-laden heart to the heart of God who invites him to Himself.

> Cast all your anxiety on him because he cares for you.
> (1 Peter 5:7)

> Come to me, all you who are weary and burdened, and I will give you rest. Take my yoke upon you and learn from me, for I am gentle and humble in heart, and you will find rest for your souls. For my yoke is easy and my burden is light. (Matthew 11:28-30)

> But I have calmed and quietened myself,
> I am like a weaned child with its mother;
> like a weaned child I am content.
> (Psalm 131:2)

Even repentance is life-giving when one is repenting to the Author of Life and the Lover of his soul. There is a sweetness known only between the repenting one and the God of Mercy which tears cannot embitter. When a repenting soul is melting in humble contrition before a welcoming God, life and peace are found.

> Godly sorrow brings repentance that leads to salvation and leaves no regret, but worldly sorrow brings death.
> (2 Corinthians 7:10)

There are many challenges to living a holy and godly life. True Life involves keeping constant watch over the heart. When a person is motivated by nothing other than the outside pressure of "do's and don'ts," disciplines and challenges are wearisome chores. He may outwardly perform the duties of a holy life, but if not moved by inward love, these performances are dead weight. But! ... when *love* motivates a life of discipline, everything changes. That love stands guard over one's heart and actions, keeping out whatever might offend and mar the precious union between the lover and the Beloved. Love disdains and hates anything which assaults its object. But it rejoices with whatever blesses its object, including those things that might be hard and challenging. When love is the motivator, not only are the obvious commands happily obeyed, but the lover actually delights to find the secret things, the hidden nuances which will bring delight to the Beloved. Love is actually ingenious in discovering the wants and delights of its object. Love changes even the harshest duties into delightful offerings.

True love does not just do the bare minimum, but goes beyond the maximum. It does not just want to "make sure Hell is escaped," but wants to pursue Heaven and the heart of God for all it's worth.

> ... and find out what pleases the Lord. Have nothing to do with the fruitless deeds of darkness, but rather expose them.
> (Ephesians 5:10,11)

Think about champion athletes or accomplished musicians. They make sacrifices today for joy tomorrow. They not only do what is required, but go well beyond. They forego not only detrimental pleasures, but many good pleasures which others seem to enjoy at will. Why? Why all this discipline? The answer is that they are held captive. Something bigger than they are has them in its grip. They are the willing servants of a desired treasure. *And*, they do all this for an *earthly* reward!

> Do you not know that in a race all the runners run, but only one gets the prize? Run in such a way as to get the prize. Everyone who competes in the games goes into strict train-ing. They do it to get a crown that will not last; but we do it to get a crown that will last for ever. (1 Corinthians 9:23-25)

LOVING GOD SIMPLIFIES LIFE

One more thing: Loving God supremely, treasuring Christ above all else, simplifies life. I did not say it makes it *easy* but *simple*. Decisions lose their complexity when your heart is motivated supremely by love of God. Remember Shadrach and his friends (Daniel 3)? When faced with the king's idol and the order to bow before it, they had no dilemma. They did not have to pray about it! "No!" "We will not bow!" Simple. Likewise Joseph when faced with Potiphar's wife and her illicit offer (Genesis 39). There was nothing for the young man to deliberate or pray about! "No!" "I will not sin against God [my Treasure]!" Simple. When Jesus is the treasure of you life, certain things become fixed and not up for negotiation. Life is simplified, even if the choice brings you into a tough situation.

LOVE TOWARDS OTHERS

We have seen that True Life is first of all defined by our love towards God (which is but a response of His to us). But True Life does not stop there! After loving God we turn to our neighbor. Love towards God and then our neighbor sums up the entire law of God.

> Hearing that Jesus had silenced the Sadducees, the Pharisees got together. One of them, an expert in the law, tested him with this question: "Teacher, which is the greatest commandment in the Law?"
>
> Jesus replied: "Love the Lord your God with all your heart and with all your soul and with all your mind." This is the first and greatest commandment. And the second is like it: "Love your neighbour as yourself." All the Law and the Prophets hang on these two commandments. (Matthew 22: 34-40)

THE SUPERNATURAL PROGRESS OF LOVE IN THE SOUL

God works miraculous changes in the life of every child of grace. Nowhere is this more evident than in the growth of love in the heart. This growth can actually be observed and measured.

First, the Christian is brought to a place where he rightly loves himself. No longer a slave to guilt and shame, he now has a sober, balanced love for himself as one loved and redeemed by God.

Then, he finds growing within the miracle of love towards his neighbour: "Love your neighbour as yourself" (Matthew 22: 39). This is truly God's work! To have love grow where once only hate once had place is sure evidence of True Life!

Next, love goes beyond loving others *as* we love ourselves, to actually *preferring* others before ourselves: " Be devoted to one another in love. Honour one another above yourselves." (Romans 12:10). To honour and prefer another over yourself is so against nature, but God *in us* makes this possible!

Finally, love grows to a place where we actually love others with the very love of Jesus: "My command is this: love each other as I have loved you." (John 15:12). Wonder of wonders! Loving others *as we have been loved* by Jesus!

It is God who will work this miracle of love within you! Trust Him to do it and expect nothing less than divine love the grow within you.

THE WONDERS OF LOVE TOWARDS OTHERS

We need not try to prove the goodness of this grace, for it is wonderfully obvious. What can be more wonderful or right than a heart that longs to embrace the whole of mankind, even the world itself with love which is sourced in God and flows out to others? When one is filled with God's love and it spills over to others, one cannot help but prefer the interests of others above his own. This is supernatural and counter to our fallen, selfish nature. When you love your neighbor as yourself, you cannot think ill of him or act wickedly toward him. You would rather endure a thousand wrongs against yourself than perpetrate one wrong against him. A person who loves others is never happier than when he is a channel of blessing and benefit to someone else. The love God gives us for others is stronger than any malice they may have toward us. Hatred cannot resist love forever. When we consistently overlook the injuries others cause us and pity their foolishness, we overcome their evil with good (Romans 12:21).

Love refuses revenge upon our enemies and instead directs all possible love upon them (Romans 12:19). Invariably, though perhaps over a long time, the one who loves others as he loves himself wins the admiration of others. A benign spirit (a heart full of love) even goes so far as to produce a sweetness to the countenance which makes the lover beautiful to all. It also brings strength of character to the inner depths of the lover, inspiring creativity and nobility that will affect every part of his life.

When you are secure in the perfect love of God, then you are free to love imperfect people who may not readily return your love, or who may actually mistreat you. You can even *bless* those who abuse you because your heart is safe in a greater love.

Think about the great heroes of history. Invariably their lives have been motivated by a love for country or colleagues, family or friend. We admire their actions, but we need to realize the hearts behind those actions. Imagine the effect for good if you – and others – were moved by a greater love for all mankind! Only the supernatural presence of God in the heart of a Christian can manifest such love.

THE JOY OF LOVING YOUR NEIGHBOUR

What a blessing it is to be set free from the poisons of malice, hatred, and envy! To have your heart swell with love toward others is sweetness to the soul. It is a delight to the whole person to be filled with love for others. To trade soul poisons for love, bitterness for sweetness, is to promote not only blessing for others, but your own happiness. If I could choose one thing that would make me happy, it would be this: to have my heart taken over with love for God, and then for every person in the entire world. Rather than envy their blessings, I would actually rejoice in them. *Their* happiness would become *my* happiness. *Their* comfort would be *my* comfort. How could I *not* want this? If my brother or sister is going through a trial, and because I love them, I feel their pain and sorrow, commiserating with them is actually far sweeter to my soul than being callous and insensible to their plight. Even in their trials, if I, in love, can point them to the deep goodness of God and remind them of the ultimate triumph of His good purposes and the certainty of eternal happiness, then I might be a source of comfort in the midst of their sorrows.

Without question, next to loving God, loving your neighbor is the greatest source of happiness. It is truly a heavenly joy experienced here and now, and when it rules in our hearts and relationships here, it actually brings the future joy of Heaven to earth.

THE EXCELLENCE OF PURITY

Remember that I named Purity as the third main branch of True Life, describing it as a true desire to say "no" to the perverse enjoyments of this fallen world and "yes" to the things that bring pleasure to our wonderful God. It embraces a resolute willingness to suffer whatever pains may come as we fulfill God's will for us. Purity is a wonderful heart attribute and brings joy and freedom.

There is perhaps no slavery so horrible as slavery to one's own lusts, and no victory so wonderful as victory over those same lusts. Never are people more miserable and debased than when sunk in the bog of their own filth. They are then incapable of living the noble lives for which they have been created and for which they have been redeemed. Enchanted with sensual pleasures, they are not free - even if they think they are. But souls possessed by True Life *know* that they were made for more! They are therefore repulsed by the temptation to step aside (off the highway of holiness) for the sake of momentary pleasure.

THE JOY OF PURITY

Purity brings joy and pleasure. People think sin brings pleasure, and it does – for a moment (Hebrews 11:25). But there is always a sting in sinful pleasure. Sinful pleasure leaves trouble strewn in its wake. Foolish excess and lustful living are enemies to the entire person's well-being, affecting both this life and the next. Just in considering the effect of intemperate living on this life alone, a wise person – one would think – will throttle back on excess and foolishness. Add to that the thought that what we do in this life affects not just time, but Eternity and there is even more motive for abhorring the poisonous pleasures of sin.

Even "innocent" pleasures, if over-pursued, can harm the health of body and soul. Therefore, the wise person pursues joy in Jesus not because he is under some law, some outward compulsion, but because he is moved by a higher pleasure. His interests have been raised, refined, and redefined so that he is no longer concerned with the things that used to captivate him. Think about this: even in the natural world, any person who is in the grip of some affection will forget about other things that would normally captivate him. He might forget his food or normal care for his body. Consider again an athlete or musician ... how their commitment to their passion relegates all other pleasures. Is it any wonder that a person caught up in True Life, being over-powered by love, should despise former pleasures that he used to adore, seeing everything now differently? He will see all lesser pleasures in their proper perspective and will not allow them to interfere with his pursuit of happiness in Jesus.

There will be challenges to face if you set out to deny yourself in the pursuit of purity of heart and life. It will not always be easy! Yet those who possess True Life find that even hardships give them an opportunity to joyfully tell of their higher love. Knowing themselves to be weak and capable of such small offerings in service to God, they see suffering as an unexpected opportunity to honour Him by bearing witness to His goodness in the midst of this life's trials.

THE EXCELLENCE OF HUMILITY

The last branch of True Life is Humility. To the untrained eye, humility is seen as a weak and despicable quality. The world laughs at it. The truth is that it is the crown of a noble soul. It is triviality and ignorance that give birth to pride. Humility is born of a higher knowledge of more meaningful things. Humility keeps the wise from loving wasteful things and being overly proud of earthly gains.

Humility actually *attracts* grace: "God opposes the proud but shows favour to the humble." (James 4:6) The noble soul has come to value Truth, and has a knowledge of what is truly valuable. He no longer judges life by money, beauty, physical strength, and such. He is not impressed by those who judge themselves as superior to others because they posses a few outward advantages. He does not look down on those who lack these temporal things. Because he now understands true value and beauty and has seen something of the wonder of the character and nature of God, he is not impressed with his former shallow attainments. He now admires a whole new world. It is the wonders and values of that world to which he now aspires.

Strange, but the value of humility can be seen by the fact that virtually everyone pretends to be humble. Very few want to be seen as arrogant and full of pride. Prideful people, desperate for praise, will be careful not to commend themselves, even while they hope others will. So often in "polite" conversation we hear people flattering others and denouncing themselves – pretending to be humble – a pretension fuelled by pride. Genuine humility must be a truly wonderful thing if it is imitated in almost every corner of social life, and considered – by the proud - to be an essential part of "good breeding"!

THE JOY AND SWEETNESS OF HUMILITY
Humility brings with it a great deal of peace. There is a sweetness that comes with a humble spirit. Conversely, the proud man, the arrogant, is not only a nuisance to all around him, but most of all he is a nuisance to himself. He is bothered by everything and content with nothing. He spends his life in a restless state of frustration. He is always ruffled. Nothing is good enough for him. He is always ready for a fight, always postured for an argument. He acts as though God Himself should do all things to attend to his pleasure, and the universe and every creature in it exists to meet his wants and wishes.

Just like the slightest wind shakes every leaf of a tall tree, so every "wind" (words, glances, expressions, etc.) agitates the proud man. He lives on the edge of torment. But think about the freedom of the humble person! When he is despised, or someone throws an offence his way, he already thinks of himself in a lowly and sober way, so he cannot be troubled by slights and offences that would torment and wound a proud man. A humble person, unlike the proud, cannot be poisoned with the everyday occurrences of life. Pride brings with it a contentious spirit that is upset by a thousand little things to which the humble are immune. The irony here is that true humility and lowliness of heart bring the honour and appreciation to the humble for which the proud are endlessly striving! The humble are loved far and wide, while the proud are beaten by their own pride, being despised by many even while living lives pretending to be honoured by all.

Since humility in the life of the believer is first and foremost expressed in relation to God, it is inevitably sweet, joy-producing, and pleasant, as is everything that relates to God in the believer's life. There is true joy in lowering yourself before your great and wonderful God. When a believer has a deep sense of God's majesty and glory, and accordingly sinks to the bottom of himself, he sees God as All and himself as nothing, and takes his rightful place. There he understands the expression of the Psalmist:

Lord, our Lord,
how majestic is your name in all the earth!
You have set your glory
in the heavens.
Through the praise of children and infants
you have established a stronghold against your enemies,
to silence the foe and the avenger.

When I consider your heavens,
the work of your fingers,
the moon and the stars,
which you have set in place,
what is mankind that you are mindful of them,
human beings that you care for them?
(Psalm 8:1-4)

A proud and ambitious person revels in the praise and applause of others, receiving their accolades with joy and pleasure. But his happiness in receiving the praise of others is not nearly so great as is the happiness of a humble soul in rejecting it.

> Not to us, Lord, not to us but to your name be the glory,
> because of your love and faithfulness. (Psalm 115:1)

I have spoken briefly, and inadequately, about the main branches of Christian Life – True Life. *Living it* will teach you more about it than my words will. As I think your soul has already been awakened to long for True Life, then go ahead and aspire to know all that God has for you! Begin by faith to pursue Life in all its fullness. Do not be afraid that God will not meet you in your pursuit of Him, for He has said:

> All those the Father gives me will come to me, and who-
> ever comes to me I will never drive away. (John 6:37)

And:

> You will seek me and find me when you seek
> me with all your heart. (Jeremiah 29:13)

PRAY THIS WITH ME

"Lord Jesus! What a wonder that You have made both my duty and my happiness to walk together as friends! In Your goodness You have determined that the "work" of guarding my soul for You shall be met with the great reward of knowing You! How can creatures as low as we be brought to such heights? What mercy! You allow *us* – welcome us – to lift our eyes to *You*. What wonder: *You* receive love and relationship from *us*! As we behold You – Your beauty, character and perfection, we actually begin to partake of Your infinite and unsurpassed blessedness, and we begin to know True Life and Joy. What a God!

Lord, I can see now that the soul which disentangles itself from all lesser loves – especially self-love – and which by the help of Your Holy Spirit places its love upon You, actually grows in health and strength and becomes truly happy. There is no happiness like that which comes from loving You above all else, and loving others for Your sake. I do truly believe, Lord Jesus, that I can never be happy until I put to death all my sinful, selfish desires and ways, conquer my pride, and learn to not love this sinful world.

But Lord! When? When will You in Your mercy come to me and do this work for me … for I cannot do it myself? I want to be satisfied in You, and as holy in You as I can be this side of Heaven! Certainly, as You have birthed this desire for Yourself in me, You will fulfill it. You have given me a glimpse of True Life. Now, Lord, when will You bring it to fullness?

Lord God, My Saviour and my Joy! Teach me to do Your will. Strengthen and establish me in Your way. You are my God and Your Spirit is good and good toward me. Complete Your work in me and Your will for me. Because Your mercy endures forever, I know that You will not forsake me, or Your plans for me, for I am the work of Your hands."

Satisfy us in the morning with your unfailing love,
that we may sing for joy and be glad
all our days.(Psalm 90:14)

Teach me your way, Lord,
that I may rely on your faithfulness;
give me an undivided heart,
that I may fear your name. (Psalm 86:11)

… Your love, Lord, endures for ever – do
not abandon the works of your hands.
(Psalm 138:8)

PART THREE

True Life Is Possible!

~

A Response to the Despondent

My Friend,

Having begun to explore the wonders of True Life, it is easy to imagine someone, with head in hands saying, "I see the beauty of Life in Christ, I see the wonders of its effect upon others, but it is too far for me! I am so swamped in sin and my own weakness. I see True Life as an impossibility! If I were asked simply to perform certain outward duties, simply to 'do' some things, I could manage this. But I am hearing here of a change on the inside, and that is something I cannot do! I can give money away to the poor. I can do any number of rites and rituals, but I cannot create a heart of love. What am I to do?"

> If I give all I possess to the poor and give over
> my body to hardship that I may boast, but do not
> have love, I gain nothing. (1 Corinthians 13:3)

"IF I COULD PAY MONEY for True Life, I would. But, the gift of God cannot be purchased with money (Acts 8:20). If I could beat my body and abuse myself, to somehow gain True Life (as many religious people do), I would. But I know that would not change my heart from worldly to heavenly ... I know I would still find many evils lurking deep within. Whatever I shut the doors to would climb in through the windows! I am well aware of the weakness and failings of my body and my soul. But rather than this making me humble, it just makes me angry and morose: Pride abounds. And, even when I do think, in some way, lowly of myself, I cannot stand it when *others* do."

"When I consider the wonders of the Life you have described, I feel like a shipwrecked man ... able to see the shore, but unable to reach it. I can see that my real problem is myself. My selfish self. I cannot get free from myself. Like a door fastened to its hinges which can swing about, but can never be free, so I can turn this way and that, but I am fast-bound by selfishness. Self-love is so deeply rooted within me that I cannot imagine that I will ever be free of it. The distance, the chasm, between me and the True Life I see in some seems impossible to cross."

THESE FEARS CAN BE OVERCOME!

These fears and thoughts are not unusual for those who have seen something of the beauty of Life in Christ. Like the spies of Israel, they have seen the beauty of the land, but they have also seen the "giants" that inhabit it (namely, "self"). They see that True Life is like a land flowing with milk and honey, but lusts and corruptions within their own hearts are like the children of Anak were to the children of Israel. They are so overcome with fear that they will never enter in and overcome the evil giants in their own hearts.

We are going to discover that there is no reason to give in to these fears. More, we should not entertain them in our thoughts or our words. If we do, it will quench the fire in our spirits, weaken our hands in our labours, and serve to strengthen our difficulties. But! We have a great big God and a wonderful Gospel!

If we are to make progress with our souls, then we must encourage ourselves with every tool that our gracious God offers us. For:

> You, dear children, are from God and have overcome them, because the one who is in you is greater than the one who is in the world. (1 John 4:4)

And:

> The eternal God is your refuge,
> and underneath are the everlasting arms.
> He will drive out your enemies before you,
> saying, "Destroy them!" (Deut. 33:27)

Our strength is *not* in ourselves, but in the Lord and in the power of His might. It is *He* that will tread down and defeat our enemies. We need to *know* that God has a tender heart and a willing disposition toward us. He *wants* us to prosper in Him. He has stated plainly that He has no pleasure in our destruction, but plans and promotes our spiritual prosperity.

> 'For I know the plans I have for you,' declares
> the Lord, 'plans to prosper you and not to harm
> you, plans to give you hope and a future.'
> (Jeremiah 29:11)

Our understanding of the nature and disposition of God is vital if we are to grow and prosper in True Life. We must be convinced, from the Bible, that there is *not a shred* of spite, envy, or malice in God towards us. His very nature is Love. It is not just an aspect of His nature, but the very essence of it.

> And so we know and rely on the love God has for us.
> God is love.
> (1 John 4:16)

God created us in a happy state. That is how we once were. Now fallen, He has put our recovery in the hands – not of an angel, archangel, nor a prophet – but of His own Son. Jesus Himself is the captain of our salvation. What enemy can overcome us when we are under the care of Him who has already conquered sin, Satan, and death?

> If God is for us, who can be against us? He who did not spare his own Son, but gave him up for us all – how will he not also, along with him, graciously give us all things? Who will bring any charge against those whom God has chosen? It is God who justifies. Who then is the one who condemns? No one. (Romans 8:31-33)

> To him who is able to keep you from stumbling and to present you before his glorious presence without fault and with great joy – to the only God our Saviour be glory, majesty, power and authority, through Jesus Christ our Lord, before all ages, now and for evermore! Amen. (Jude 24,25)

Just think: Here is the Son of God, the Eternal Son of God. Loved perfectly by His Father. It is *He* - and no one else - who leaves

Heaven and lives, tabernacles, dwells among *us*. Why? For nothing less than that He should redeem us for His Father, recover His Father's image within us, and restore us to Life. All that He did, all that He suffered, was designed deliberately for this purpose. He lived, He labored, He suffered, He bled, He died to bring glory to His Father through the recovery of us rebels.

Was this all for nothing? Have His labours been in vain? No! It is promised of Jesus:

> After he has suffered,
> he will see the light of life and be satisfied;
> by his knowledge my righteous servant will justify many,
> and he will bear their iniquities.
> (Isaiah 53:11)

It is impossible that Jesus' work for our redemption – for *your* redemption - being the very eternal plan of Heaven, should come to nothing. God's plan will not miscarry. It has already saved countless and *you* will not be God's first "abortion." Millions of others have been brought from as far away as you to fullness in Christ. He has already proven that … "He is able to save completely those who come to God through him, because he always lives to intercede for them." (Hebrews 7:25) He is a willing, tender, compassionate Saviour who knows our weaknesses and has been touched by them. Take courage in this!

> A bruised reed he will not break, and a smouldering wick he will not snuff out. (Matthew 12:20)

> As a father has compassion on his children,
> so the Lord has compassion on those who fear him;

for he knows how we are formed,
he remembers that we are dust.(Psalm 103:13,14)

Even more, our gracious and good and willing God has sent His Holy Spirit who is active to this day (as active as ever!) in awakening hearts, illuminating the Scriptures, drawing sinners to Christ, and perfecting feeble believers in Christ. It is God's Holy Spirit who gives life to the dead and softens the hearts of the hard. It is He who helps us see and understand the amazing purpose that God has for us. It is He who is ready and willing to help us weak creatures in our journey toward godliness and joy. It is He who will cherish in us the smallest spark of True Life and bring it forth into a flame. God the Holy Spirit does this! It is a *divine* work in us, not our own work. What is said in Solomon's Song of the love between a husband and his bride is surely even more true of the love that God has for each and every one of us:

> Many waters cannot quench love;
> rivers cannot sweep it away..
> (Song of Solomon 8:7)

Why should we think it to be impossible – that true love and goodness should finally conquer our hearts? When the day begins to dawn, darkness is dispelled. Always. As the light easily destroys the darkness, so the Truth easily holds sway over ignorance and folly. The corruptions of a fallen heart *must* flee from the wonders and power of the Gospel. Just as with the rising sun, so "The path of the righteous is like the morning sun, shining ever brighter till the full light of day." (Proverbs 4:18) Trust that "...as they go from strength to strength, till each appears before God in Zion ..." (Psalm 84:7), so shall you.

GOD PROMISES TO PERFECT YOU

There are so many promises in the Bible whereby God assures us that He will work in us patiently and relentlessly until the job is finished. Part of our "work" is to trust in His promises and live accordingly. His promises are not there to make us lazy and passive, but eager and active. They motivate us to action; they do not rock us to sleep!

> … being confident of this, that he who began a good work in you will carry it on to completion until the day of Christ Jesus. (Philippians 1:6)

> For by one sacrifice he has made perfect for ever those who are being made holy. (Hebrews 10:14)

> His divine power has given us everything we need for a godly life through our knowledge of him who called us by his own glory and goodness. Through these he has given us his very great and precious promises, so that through them you may participate in the divine nature, having escaped the corruption in the world caused by evil desires.
>
> For this very reason, make every effort to add to your faith goodness; and to goodness, knowledge; and to knowledge, self-control; and to self-control, perseverance; and to perseverance, godliness; and to godliness, mutual affection; and to mutual affection, love. For if you possess these qualities in increasing measure, they will keep you from being ineffective and unproductive in your knowledge of our Lord Jesus Christ. But whoever does not have them is short-sighted and blind, forgetting that they have been cleansed from their past sins. (2 Peter 1:3-9)

For those God foreknew he also predestined to be conformed to the image of his Son, that he might be the firstborn among many brothers and sisters. And those he predestined, he also called; those he called, he also justified; those he justified, he also glorified. (Romans 8:29,30)

So, open your Bible, get before God, lift your heart to Him, and let His Word ignite true faith in your heart!

Think about this: The entire human race (when it was comprised of two people, Adam and Eve) was once full of goodness and love. Sin and hate are invaders. They are not original, but are usurpers. Yes, we are all now fallen in Adam, and self-love is deeply rooted in our nature, but it was once not so. If we were "right" we would happily and fully love God and be totally devoted to Him. If we were in tune with God we would love Him infinitely more that we love ourselves, and readily comply with His will. Certainly He who made us is able – and willing - to fix us! Certainly He will help us in this fight, if we will enter into it. We too can be like those "who became powerful in battle and routed foreign armies" (Hebrews 11:34), even those enemies within our own hearts.

You will find that no sooner than you determine to enter this fight all of Heaven is there to help you! More than that, all the Church (I mean true believers) on earth is ready to support and encourage you. Christians all over the world are and will be praying for you and for your victory over sin, Satan, and self. Then there is the Church Triumphant – believers who are now in Heaven – who no doubt have an interest in your welfare and victory. The Bible seems to say this great cloud of witnesses actually intercedes before the throne of God for us (see Hebrews 12:1; Revelation 6:9,10). Just as Elisha urged his servant to open his eyes and see the armies of

Heaven arrayed in battle for them, so our eyes of faith need to be opened to see the vast help of Heaven there for us!

> Therefore, since we are surrounded by such a great cloud of witnesses, let us throw off everything that hinders and the sin that so easily entangles. And let us run with perseverance the race marked out for us, fixing our eyes on Jesus, the pioneer and perfecter of faith. For the joy that was set before him he endured the cross, scorning its shame, and sat down at the right hand of the throne of God. Consider him who endured such opposition from sinners, so that you will not grow weary and lose heart. (Hebrews 12:1-3)

WE ARE ACTIVE IN THIS, BUT SO IS GOD

So, away with all the fears – and excuses! The battle is more than half won once we see God's heart in this matter. Christ bought our pardon on the Cross, but He also bought our sanctification. When we see God's heart, then we can determine, by the grace of God, to work and to pray, to war and to rely, to fight and to trust, to labour and to lean, to do our part and to trust God to do His part. We are not passive, but neither are we alone in this endeavor: "Now begin the work, and the Lord be with you." (1 Chronicles 22:16)

Do not be confused here: Salvation is of the Lord. He does it. We cannot do one thing to atone for our sins. We cannot pay the price to ransom ourselves. And it is God who stirs our hearts and brings us to new life in Christ. We do not do this ourselves. God sovereignly and graciously does it. We receive the pardon of our sins simply by faith, and are justified by our gracious, holy God. Likewise, we receive our sanctification (we grow in Christ-likeness) by faith, trusting the promise of God to work in us, and trusting Him to *empower us to action.*

So, in the onward growth of our souls, we are not passive. Faith is active trust. Faith does not induce laziness, but produces action. That is why in the pursuit of a holy character the Bible describes the Christian life with words like "wrestle," "run," "watch," and "diligence." We, in the end, are as holy and happy as we want to be. If we lie about, passively waiting for God to do what He has commanded and enabled us to do, we will never make progress. We should apply the same diligence and effort to our Christian progress as an athlete, a soldier, or a farmer does in theirs (*c.f.* 2 Timothy 2:1-7) confident that God gives all grace for what He commands.

Take an example from the world around us. We cannot make the smallest flower. We cannot make one stalk of wheat. Only God can. All of our effort and wits cannot create something from nothing.

He makes grass grow for the cattle. (Psalm 104:14)

But who would therefore suggest that we do not need the work of the farmer to take what God has created and husband it into abundance?

And plants for people to cultivate. (Psalm 104:14)

Likewise, only God can form the child in the womb. It is He who creates the miracle of life. Only He can create a soul. But who can deny that He has also ordained the marriage bed as the means to bring that life into existence, and the nurture and wisdom of parents to bring that life to adult stature?

So, God must, with sovereign grace and power, impart Life into a dead soul. He alone can do this. He does it through the hearing of the Gospel and the work of the Holy Spirit. Yet we must then stir

ourselves to respond to His awakening. In a sense it is like responding to an alarm clock. We are passive in the sense that God alone
can awaken the soul, doing the miraculous secret inner work. But
then we are active in responding. Pictures of this balance between
the sovereign work of God and our active response are everywhere
in the Bible:

> Then he said to the man, 'Stretch out your hand.' So he
> stretched it out and it was completely restored, just as sound
> as the other. (Matthew 12: 13)

> Then Jesus said to him, 'Get up! Pick up your mat and walk.'
> At once the man was cured; he picked up his mat and walked.
> (John 5:8,9)

> But by the grace of God I am what I am, and his grace to
> me was not without effect. No, I worked harder than all of
> them – yet not I, but the grace of God that was with me. (1
> Corinthians 15:10)

In the initial work of saving sinners there are times when God
overwhelms the unwilling - standing in their way, taking hold of
them and stopping their wayward course. The obvious example is
Saul (soon to be Paul) on the road to Damascus. As far as we can
tell, there seemed to be no movement toward God in Paul. God
overwhelmed him. But "normally" - even in the first moment of
conversion - God uses "means": The preacher preaches and commands the sinner to repent. The sinner responds, turns, repents,
comes, believes. God is working where only He can, but man is
obeying by responding. We see the outward, but God is doing the
inward.

If responding in active obedience is needed in the first moments of salvation, how much more is our response to God's workings needed in the onward growth of our souls!

HOW DO WE DEVELOP TRUE LIFE?

So, my next happy duty is to show the course we need to take in order to see this precious Life develop within us. I am glad to say that I have not the complete and only truth in this matter. You will find others that will help, others who have wisdom. Just like a given physician may prescribe one remedy and another may prescribe another equally effective, so there are helps and there is wisdom beyond me! However, it is my hope that what I share will help you, even as others might find help with another's advice. God has more than one way to deal with the souls of men and women, as we all differ one from another. We should not be upset or disquieted therefore if we find help in a way not exactly prescribed or used by another.

So, I want you to see a real freedom in what follows. Yes, there is an order to it, but this is not law or legalism. This is not a recipe. We are not baking a cake; we are helping one another on the course to fullness in Christ. Yet, the following pieces do fit together, and if applied with diligence, as you are able, will serve to help you on the way to True Life.

There is a *deliberateness* about what follows. Just as you will not get fit while sitting on the sofa with a box of donuts, so you will not gain Life while your focus is on trivial things. You will not go deep by splashing around in the shallows. There needs to be a resolve, an intention, a desperation. Grace is not available to make us lazy and cover our excuses, but to empower us and enable us to do what is otherwise impossible and out of our natural reach.

So! Take courage and let's get started!

BEFORE ALL ELSE, TURN FROM ALL MANNER OF SIN

If we are serious in this pursuit of a holy and godly life, if we do truly want to honour God and live for His glory, if it really is our desire to have our lives conformed to His will and His Image fully formed within us, then we *must* declare war against the sins which we not only outwardly commit, but those which reside secretly in our hearts. There must be true resolve here! There must be diligent care here! There must be a deliberate turning and moving away from sin in its every form. You *cannot* "cut corners" here. But you *can* cry out to God for His supernatural help: "Have mercy on me, O God, according to your unfailing love; … Create in me a pure heart, O God, and renew a steadfast spirit within me." (Psalm 51:1,10). You will find all of Heaven on your side once you resolve to get tough on your sins!

True Repentance is serious business! It is violent and radical. Times of repentance are times of crisis. They are defining moments:

> And if your foot causes you to stumble, cut it off. It is better for you to enter life crippled than to have two feet and be thrown into hell. And if your eye causes you to stumble, pluck it out. It is better for you to enter the kingdom of God with one eye than to have two eyes and be thrown into hell, where "the worms that eat them do not die, and the fire is not quenched." (Mark 9:45-48)

But repentance leads to Life!

> Godly sorrow brings repentance that leads to salvation and leaves no regret … (2 Corinthians 7:10)

We dare not, we cannot, make any treaty with sin. We must lay down every weapon of rebellion. There can be no softness here. Every willful sin is a deep and dangerous wound to the soul. Sin is poison, and we cannot expect any spiritual health if we are at the same time poisoning our souls. Sin distances us from God and all of His good plans for us. If our hands are dirty, our hearts will be defiled as well. (In other words, we cannot apply the false comfort that even though we are doing wrong, our hearts are good. Hearts and hands are vitally and always connected.)

Now, I will admit that temptations are strong. I will admit that our natures are vile and corrupt. But I will not admit that resisting sin and temptation is an impossibility. We still have *some* power in our bodies to control where our feet take us and where our hands go. We have some control over our tongues, thoughts, and fantasies. We are *not* totally helpless and therefore excusable! If we actually began to exercise the muscles of resistance, we would find them getting stronger and temptations getting weaker. But we have to *want* this! It will require a total commitment of ourselves and our wills; it will require watchfulness and care if – even in a natural sense – we are to exercise our powers as far as can be. Many would rather hide behind the excuse of "I cannot help it!"

TREASURING JESUS IS THE SECRET TO HATING SIN

When you sin, you are in reality saying, "Jesus, right now, I love and treasure this sin more than I do You." The opposite of loving sin is loving Jesus. The power of His love in us is greater than the power of sin over us. So, the secret is not "trying harder" but "treasuring higher." It is as we treasure Christ - His love for us and our response of love back to Him – *above* any and all else, including sin, that we find new power over old sins. As one has observed, the love of God (and I would add, our love relationship back to God) has an *expulsive power* over sin. It can push it out of our lives.

If you want to break the power of sin in your life, open you Bible, lift your heart to Heaven and ask the Holy Spirit to show you the glory of Jesus in His Book. Make it your aim to get to a place where you are seeing and savouring your Saviour in His Word ... a place where your relationship with Him is more valuable to you than all treasure in all the world and more pleasurable the greatest pleasure of any sin. Treasuring higher will do your soul more good than a lifetime of trying harder.

> How then could I do such a wick-
> ed thing and sin against God?
> (Joseph to Potiphar's wife, Genesis 39:9)

KNOW YOUR ENEMY! WE NEED TO IDENTIFY SIN

If we are going to fight sin, we need to be sure that we know just what it is. In identifying sin, we dare not take advice from those around us or from the common opinion of society – even those we think of as "good people." Most of us have a very light view of sin, especially our own. As a matter of fact, to some the only real sin is being precise about sin! Unless something is what society might call a "gross sin" (and that definition changes with fashion), most do not recognize things as sinful which are in fact deadly to the soul. We tend to allow ourselves a lot of slack where our sins are concerned.

Most of us embrace much pride and vanity. We allow foolishness and filth in our behavior and speech. Even if we do see such as sin, our progress against it is often slowed to a crawl, and our victories are few. It is apparent that we need a better strategy!

First, we need to recognize that we each must answer for our-selves before God, and it will do no good on that day to say "Well, Bill did it!" or "I was better than some!" "For we must all appear be-fore the judgment seat of Christ, so that each of us may receive what is due to us for the things done while in the body, whether good or bad." (2 Corinthians 5:10).

It is foolish – really foolish – to judge ourselves by any standard other than that by which we will be judged. If we are ever going to sort ourselves out, and straighten out our paths it will be only by taking heed to the Word of God (*c.f.* Psalm 119:9). It is because the Word of God is quick, sharp, active, able to penetrate and discern (*c.f.* Hebrews 4:12) that it alone is able to search our depths and bring to light things hidden in darkness and otherwise impossible for us to see, and perhaps accepted as fine in the eyes of others.

> Though people tried to bribe me,
> I have kept myself from the ways of the violent
> through what your lips have commanded.
> (Psalm 17:4)

If we hated sin as much as we hated sickness, we would live better lives. Like a little cough that foretells a grave illness, so a little sin can fore-tell a future of woe. We can know where sin begins, but we can never know where it will end. The Prodigal had no thought of a pigsty when he boldly strode away from his father's house. Samson's little indiscre-tions led him to lose more than his eyesight … he lost God's presence in his life. The list can go on and on: Judas, Demas, Balaam. Sin is serious; sin is deadly. It is worthy of our greatest hatred.

We need to know what God thinks! We need to know His mind as He has shown it to us in His Word. We need to know what Jesus has to say and what the apostles say. We need to read and submit to our Bibles, *and* prayerfully ask God to convict our hearts of *anything* displeasing to Him. Only then, if we do it with an honest intention, will we know the mind of God regarding sin. Then having discovered what God thinks about sin, we need to decide that we are *never again* going to look upon sin as a light and harmless thing. We are not going to joke about it and treat it as though it is unimportant. In fact, we need to be fully persuaded that the smallest sin is infinitely wicked and dangerous. The smallest sin has lethal power to the soul as the smallest tumour has to the body. No one will be happy with a "little" cancer. They want it out! They see its danger if left alone! If we were thinking right, we would be as disturbed by the smallest sins as we are by the biggest crimes. Both are infinitely vile in the eyes of God, and both have the power to ruin a soul!

CONSIDERING WHERE SIN WILL TAKE US WILL HELP US TO RESIST IT

When God shows us things that are sinful, we will see that some of them have been very dear to us. We have loved some of them for a long time! We have learned to take comfort in some of them. Some of them are so precious to us that we only bring them out on special occasions! That is why Jesus says that repentance can be so very painful - even maiming - to our sinful selves. Again:

> And if your eye causes you to stumble, pluck it out. It is better for you to enter the kingdom of God with one eye than to have two eyes and be thrown into hell … (Mark 9:47)

So, should we wait – cherishing our sins - until it is easy to repent and be done with them? Will it be easier to remove a cancer tomorrow - when it is bigger - than today? It will never be easier than today to get on with this! Don't be like little children who will hang onto a plaything until they are tired of it and only then let it go. Sin does not work that way. It sticks to us. It goes deeper into us each time we indulge. Nor should we wait passively for God to change us and make it easy for us, when all the time He is urging us to get on and deal with it.

God is ready to help us! His Holy Spirit will empower our feeble effort and add strength to our weak repentance. We should never be reluctant to have sin exposed, because Jesus is an expert at cleansing sin from our hearts! Be willing to have it discovered and ready to repent!

> If we claim to be without sin, we deceive ourselves and the truth is not in us. If we confess our sins, he is faithful and just and will forgive us our sins and purify us from all unrighteousness. (1John 1:8,9)

Let's just suppose for a minute that we have no higher motivation to repent than a desire to escape Hell. Let's imagine that we are not moved by a higher principle like the love of God, or a desire to see Him glorified in our lives. Well, let that selfish motive – the desire to avoid the horrid consequences of sin - give us a shove toward repentance. If selfishness made us pursue sinful pleasure, let it help us turn from those pleasures that we might avoid the punishment which sin inevitably brings. Fight selfishness with its own weapon, at least for the start. It will never do you any harm to stop and think about the offense your sin has caused to our sin-hating God, and what a fearful thing it is to finally anger a patient God. You will never be wrong to consider the fact that your whole existence hangs and depends upon God's incredible mercy, and all

He has to do is give you what you deserve, and you will be miserable forever.

People do not want to think like this, but they should, and we must if we will make progress away from sin and death and toward True Life.

We need to think often about the brevity of our lives and the nearness of death. Just a few more turns of the earth, a few more conversations, a few more joys and sorrows, and we will all – every one of us – be laid in a dark and cold grave. If we have not repented, we will take with us unimaginable anguish and regret for all of our offensive enjoyments. Take some time and think about the misery of a guilty soul, finding itself defenseless, with no Saviour, exposed before the Holy, impartial and severe Judge: Standing there to give an account, not only of the big things, but of every word uttered and every thought considered.

> But I tell you that everyone will have to give account on the day of judgment for every empty word they have spoken. (Matthew 12:36)

> You have set our iniquities before you, our secret sins in the light of your presence. (Psalm 90:8)

How we need Jesus!

We will do well to often think about our final day in this life. That will help us live well today. More than that, we should often ponder the time when history as we know it will close. There will be a day when the very foundations of the earth will be shaken: "But the day of the Lord will come like a thief. The heavens will disappear with a roar; the elements will be destroyed by fire, and the earth and everything done in it will be laid bare." (2 Peter 3:10). Then we will see – with our own eyes – our precious Lord Jesus. The very One who came into this world in lowliness and humility to pay for our sin and ransom us from sin, Satan, and death will appear – not in humility – but in majesty, in flaming fire. Then He will avenge all the wrongs of His enemies and deal with all who have thought they had cast Him off. ... "Wait until the Lord comes. He will bring to light what is hidden in darkness and will expose the motives of the heart." (1 Corinthians 4;5).

Then, on that day – think about this – the secret sins, the little frauds, which the world never imagined to be in us, shall be exposed and open for all to see. Thousands of actions, words, and intentions, which we never thought of as being sinful will be brought home to our – fully awakened – consciences. At that time our conviction of guilt will be so plain for us and all to see that there will be no point in arguing our case or cause.

Every angel in Heaven, and every believer who ever lived on earth will approve the dreadful sentence of our Holy God. Wickedness will be so evident that even those who have loved wickedness supremely will agree with God – their senses finally awake – that they deserve punishment. Thus they will make no appeal, but, hating what they once loved, they will agree with God against themselves.

Jesus Christ speaks of eternal punishment in the most graphic terms. Here is the One who is the sinner's friend. Yet He uses the strongest metaphors to describe the indescribable. We should pay close attention to His warnings and think about the images and pictures He presses upon us. ... All the while remembering that the reality will be worse than the metaphor. As unpleasant as this subject is, as distasteful it is to talk and think about, the experience of it will be far worse than any discussion now. If we cannot handle *this*, how do we think we will handle *that*? The hope is that in seeing how

Jesus describes judgment and punishment in the Bible we might be frightened and persuaded to change our course. Why else would Jesus have warned us in such graphic ways? As much as we love our sins, and fond as we are of our rebellion against God, the contemplation of eternal wrath ought to make us turn around!

> Do not be afraid of those who kill the body but can-
> not kill the soul. Rather, be afraid of the One
> who can destroy both soul and body in hell.
> (Matthew 10:28)

There was a rich man who was dressed in purple and fine linen and lived in luxury every day. At his gate was laid a beggar named Lazarus, covered with sores and longing to eat what fell from the rich man's table. Even the dogs came and licked his sores.

The time came when the beggar died and the angels carried him to Abraham's side. The rich man also died and was buried. In Hades, where he was in torment, he looked up and saw Abraham far away, with Lazarus by his side. So he called to him, "Father Abraham, have pity on me and send Lazarus to dip the tip of his finger in water and cool my tongue, because I am in agony in this fire."

But Abraham replied, "Son, remember that in your lifetime you received your good things, while Lazarus received bad things, but now he is comforted here and you are in agony. And besides all this, between us and you a great chasm has been set in place, so that those who want to go from here to you cannot, nor can anyone cross over from there to us."

He answered, "Then I beg you, father, send Lazarus to my family, for I have five brothers. Let him warn them, so that they will not also come to this place of torment." (Luke 16:19-28)

Why do you think the Bible, the book that speaks more of love (and especially of God's love) than any other book, speaks so passionately about wrath and Hell if not to pull us away from the sins we love, which God hates? The descriptions in the Bible are calculated to influence not just the Christian mind, but the most carnal mind. It is (no doubt) true that fear of Hell cannot make a person truly good, nor can it transform the heart. But it can be used to restrain and awaken, paving the road for a better message of love and grace.

WE MUST BE WATCHFUL OVER OURSELVES AT ALL TIMES

Now, it will do no good at all to think of these things, to be moved by the consideration of them, and to even make some determined choices regarding them, if we do not see the need to stand guard over ourselves at all times. This is non-negotiable! "Above all else, guard your heart, for everything you do flows from it." (Proverbs 4:23). Many are stirred, aroused, awakened – but only for a little while. Before long they fall asleep, as it were, and lose eternal perspective once again. It is right then, when our guard is down, that the Tempter strikes. There comes the "knock-knock" upon our doors, and sometimes we can open them even before we are aware that it is the hater of our souls who is wanting in! So many of us, like fools, live the fast life of "adventure" (so-called), scarcely awake to the dangers all about us, taking little or no thought for what we think, say, do, where we go, or the company we keep.

This is very serious business. If we would move beyond just a few fleeting impulses to "do better," wanting instead True Life thriving within us, we need to pay careful attention to our ways. We need to study our hearts and get to know their impulses and motives. Where do our passions come from and where are they headed? What is prompting a particular act or thought or word? Will it glorify God, better self, and benefit others? We need to learn to live in vital awareness that we are always in the presence of God. We need to have an eye on Him who has His eyes always upon us. We need to be aware – really aware – of the fact that we are encompassed by His light. There are no dark corners where we can hide filth –not from Him.

This reality needs to become our habitual thought life. The conscious sense of the Ever-Present God is both the greatest deterrent to sin and the greatest discoverer of it. Whatever excuses you or I can make, however we can make sin palatable, we don't dare to look God straight in the face with our excuses. If we look to Him, He will shine His light upon us. He will instruct us, correct us, and lead us.

You have searched me, LORD,
and you know me.
You know when I sit and when I rise;
you perceive my thoughts from afar.
You discern my going out and my lying down;
you are familiar with all my ways.

Before a word is on my tongue
you, LORD, know it completely.
You hem me in behind and before,
and you lay your hand upon me.
Such knowledge is too wonderful for me,
too lofty for me to attain.

Where can I go from your Spirit?
here can I flee from your presence?
If I go up to the heavens, you are there;
if I make my bed in the depths, you are there.

If I rise on the wings of the dawn,
if I settle on the far side of the sea,
even there your hand will guide me,
your right hand will hold me fast.

If I say, 'Surely the darkness will hide me
and the light become night around me,'
even the darkness will not be dark to you;
the night will shine like the day,
for darkness is as light to you.

For you created my inmost being;
you knit me together in my mother's womb.
I praise you because I am fearfully and wonderfully made;
your works are wonderful,
I know that full well.

My frame was not hidden from you
when I was made in the secret place,
when I was woven together in the depths of the earth.
Your eyes saw my unformed body;
all the days ordained for me were written in your book
before one of them came to be.

How precious to me are your thoughts, O God!
How vast is the sum of them!

Were I to count them,
they would outnumber the grains of sand –
when I awake, I am still with you.

If only you, God, would slay the wicked!
Away from me, you who are bloodthirsty!
They speak of you with evil intent;
your adversaries misuse your name.

Do I not hate those who hate you, Lord,
and abhor those who are in rebellion against you?
I have nothing but hatred for them;
I count them my enemies.

Search me, God, and know my heart;
test me and know my anxious thoughts.
See if there is any offensive way in me,
and lead me in the way everlasting.
(Psalm 139)

We Need to Regularly Examine our Actions

Taking care over ourselves is not some "deluxe" version of the Christian Life. It is necessary for all who will prosper in their walk with the Lord. The way of carelessness is the way to destruction. It is the way of the hardened conscience. The way to Life is the path of the careful and the way of the tender conscience. We need to learn to be as diligent with our souls as we are with our finances, our hobbies, our homes, our careers. This involves checking and examining our thoughts and our actions. We will often see sins that we had before glossed over and ignored. There will be many trips to the cross, many times of humble confession and repentance. There will be tears, but tears of repentance are always followed by joy! Times of self-examination will be times that strengthen our resolve to leave off the old ways and follow hard after God. Such times will help us to understand just how sin gained ground on us, so we can develop strategies against temptation and against Satan's tactics in the future.

Wise and diligent followers of Jesus have often taken time at the end of each day to take stock of that day's living and of their hearts (even as a banker will take stock at the end of a day's affairs). We can then not only take comfort in the victories of that day, but we can correct its failings, confess our sins before God's throne of grace, be comforted in the Gospel before we sleep, and mark out a safer and better course for tomorrow.

We can see in all of this that virtuous living is an art, and requires deliberate decision and action. But doing these things will greatly advance the work of Jesus in us, and increasingly give us victories in the battle for purity. This is really no different than what a serious athlete will do, or a musician, or a soldier bent on victory.

In all of this, do not forget to pray! We will make no progress without the supernatural help of our gracious God. And do not wait until you have made your own progress before you feel that you can ask God for His help. Start crying out to Him now. Have at least as much concern for gaining holiness as you do for avoiding the common calamities of life. The sins that seem to so easily gain ground on you will not leave without God's power. And even if your prayer life still has much to be desired, and your heart is feeble, what stirring there is will make your weak prayer that much more earnest. If God cares for the birds of the air, then certainly He will hear the faint cries of a faltering disciple, even if they come from no higher motive than wanting to avoid Hell. More, your prayers against sin will actually strengthen your own resolve to battle. *Our* hearts will be affected as we cry to *His* heart! Common sense will tell you that you are less likely to embrace a sin in this moment from which you have in the last moment cried to God for deliverance.

Friend! Run *to* Jesus at the first moment of temptation! Our enemy will lie to you and tell you that Jesus will not have you when you are struggling, that He only wants "victorious followers." But when we are desperate and needy that is when He wants us the most. He is at His best (for us) when we are at our worst (for Him)!

> Therefore, since we have a great high priest who has ascended into heaven, Jesus the Son of God, let us hold firmly to the faith we profess. For we do not have a high priest who is unable to feel sympathy for our weaknesses, but we have one who has been tempted in every way, just as we are – yet he did not sin. Let us then approach God's throne of grace with confidence, so that we may receive mercy and find grace to help us in our time of need. (Hebrews 4:14-16)

The Unavoidable Law of Sowing and Reaping

Friend, no one, not you, not I, can avoid the law of sowing and reaping. You cannot plant bad things into your life and expect to reap good things. If you want to gain Life, then you *must* plant life-giving seeds within. What you watch, what you read, what you hear, the company you keep, all these "seeds" will – without fail – produce from their kind either Life or Death. It is foolishness and presumption to expect to live carelessly and be happy in Jesus. Learn to sow seeds of Life if you want to harvest Life! Get rid of all bad seeds as surely and ruthlessly as a farmer destroys noxious seeds.

Do not be deceived: God cannot be mocked. A man reaps what he sows. Whoever sows to please their flesh, from the flesh will reap destruction; whoever sows to please the Spirit, from the Spirit will reap eternal life. Let us not become weary in doing good, for at the proper time we will reap a harvest if we do not give up. (Galatians 6:7-9)

Finally, brothers and sisters, whatever is true, whatever is noble, whatever is right, whatever is pure, whatever is lovely, whatever is admirable – if anything is excellent or praiseworthy – think about such things. Whatever you have learned or received or heard from me, or seen in me – put it into practice. And the God of peace will be with you. (Philippians 4:8,9)

THERE IS VALUE IN SELF-RESTRAINT EVEN OVER LAWFUL THINGS

We need to have mastery over our appetites and urges. It is obvious that we should avoid sin if we are to pursue Life. But wisdom will teach us that if we are to gain mastery over unlawful things, then it is helpful to learn to master *all* urges and desires, including those that are not sinful. In short, we need to be the master of ourselves. Only then will the strength of our natural selves be subdued under the rule of our spiritual selves.

'I have the right to do anything,' you say – but not everything is beneficial. 'I have the right to do anything'– but I will not be mastered by anything.

(1 Corinthians 6:12)

Sometimes wise parents will subdue the wills of their children by opposing them even in seemingly small matters, so that when they grow they will be trainable in bigger matters. So we should be training ourselves in little things (i.e. eating habits and sleeping habits) so that we can have mastery over more crucial things (i.e. sexuality and money habits).

If you want mastery over pride and vanity, then learn to not hear, solicit, or love the just and deserved praises of your peers for things well done. And when you are being corrected by others, learn to take it, even if you feel that you have every reason to argue your case and present your innocence.

Learn to not defend yourself by speaking to others in a spirit of revenge. Deny yourself the satisfaction of telling others of how you have been mistreated by this or that person. If we want to learn not to sin with our words, then we need to learn to hold our peace and to speak little until we have true command over that unruly dangerous tongue. ... "Many words mark the speech of a fool." (Ecclesiastes 5:3)

> ... Christ suffered for you, leaving you an example, that you should follow in his steps.

> 'He committed no sin,
> and no deceit was found in his mouth.'

> When they hurled their insults at him, he did not retaliate; when he suffered, he made no threats. Instead, he entrusted himself to him who judges justly. (1 Peter 2:21-23)

So, we should learn to put a rope around our natural drives and inclinations, letting them get used to "no." In so doing we will find that we are bringing our whole natural selves into obedience to a higher master.

WE NEED TO MAKE EVERY EFFORT TO FALL OUT OF LOVE WITH THE WORLD

It is so easy to be attached to the things of this life. Certainly God has given us all good things to enjoy in their proper place. But it is dangerously easy to put too much of our affection and attention on things which will not last. And it is a fact that the more we are consumed with the things of this life, the more depressed our spirits become, the slower our walk toward Heaven becomes, and the more sluggish our hearts become toward God. The first step in freeing ourselves from the "over-love" of this world is convincing ourselves – truly being persuaded – of the emptiness, vanity, and inability of this world, even at its best, to satisfy the heart. Remember Solomon's bitter experience:

> I undertook great projects: I built houses for myself and planted vineyards. I made gardens and parks and planted all kinds of fruit trees in them. I made reservoirs to water groves of flourishing trees. I bought male and female slaves and had other slaves who were born in my house. I also owned more herds and flocks than anyone in Jerusalem before me. I amassed silver and gold for myself, and the treasure of kings and provinces. I acquired male and female singers, and a harem[j] as well – the delights of a man's heart. I became greater by far than anyone in Jerusalem before me. In all this my wisdom stayed with me. I denied myself nothing my eyes desired; I refused my heart no pleasure. My heart took delight in all my labour, and this was the reward for all my toil.

Yet when I surveyed all that my hands had done and what I had toiled to achieve, everything was meaningless, a chasing after the wind; nothing was gained under the sun. …

So I hated life, because the work that is done under the sun was grievous to me. All of it is meaningless, a chasing after the wind.
(Ecclesiastes 2:4-11, 17)

It is very easy to say that we love Christ above all else, and that we are not in love with this world and its ways. Such words can roll off our tongues with ease, especially when we are talking with our Christian friends. We are supposed to say that! But down deeper, our hearts have little feeling for what our mouths are so easily saying. We can say that all the things of this world are "nothing," yet these "nothings" take up nearly all of our time, thoughts, energy, and talents! These "nothings" – which we claim not to hold too dear - dampen our love for God and things eternal and endlessly trick us into sin after sin.

On a good day we can make some sort of resolution against a particular worldly joy, and brush it off. But often these resolutions are shallow. No sooner have we made them than the vain thing is knocking at the door again - if not the front door, then the back door. Our half-hearted turnings don't stop the world flattering us in some other way, still hoping that we will offer it our affections. We might go through this many times, each circumstance being slightly altered enough to fool us into thinking it will be different this time. Only when we get a true and serious contempt for the things of this world will we once and for all begin to make progress in our war against loving them.

The human soul is a very vigorous thing! It seems to have an inexhaustible thirst for meaning and fulfillment. It can be likened to a raging fire! It is always reaching for something that will bring it satisfaction and peace. But! If it could be truly ripped away from the lower things of this world, with all their bewitching, empty promises, it would waste no time in searching for the higher enjoyments for which it has been created. It would soon find satisfaction – not in the glittering vanities of this life – but in nothing less than God Himself. There alone the delivered soul would find such beauty and sweetness that would captivate its love and attention forever.

It is simply impossible to love God and love the world at the same time. By "the world" I do not mean the sunset and the birdsong. I mean the values of a fallen culture. Jesus said it plainly: "No one can serve two masters. Either you will hate the one and love the other, or you will be devoted to the one and despise the other." (Matthew 6:24)

The Bible tells us not to love the world: "Do not love the world or anything in the world. If anyone loves the world, love for the Father is not in them." (1 John 2:15) There is a plain contrast here. We cannot love God and the values of a fallen, rebel world.

Again this does not mean that we do not value and appreciate the good things God has created and given to us. It is the over-valuing of them, the idolizing of them, and the fascination with things that God forbids. Just like a scale rises and falls as one side outweighs the other, so our affections for God or the world rise and fall in relation to each other. True Life languishes as false love flourishes, and True Life thrives when love is rightly placed in The Eternal.

We can easily see, therefore, that it is the duty of a Christian to battle for godly and heavenly affection in his heart. Think this through and you can literally reason your way out of foolish low-level love. Convince yourself – at a deep level – of the futility of the love of things, and of their inability to satisfy the heart. Look at the emptiness of others who love this world too much (Remember Solomon as "Exhibit *A*"). Look at the fullness of those who have fixed their hearts above. Consider these things. Examine your own heart and discover for yourself when you have been truly happiest. Ponder, over and over until you are truly and thoroughly convinced of the value of loving and treasuring God above all else.

In the midst of your busy pursuits, stop and ask ... don't go soft on yourself here ... "Why am I doing this? What is my goal in all of this? Can the muddy waters of lust and sensuality produce purity of Joy? Can the affection and applause of silly fallen creatures produce the lasting meaning and pleasure for which my heart was created? Can the irrational and temporary satisfy the longings of a rational and eternal being? Haven't I tried it all already (and if I haven't others around me have!)? Will the vain things the world keeps running after suddenly deliver a joy and fullness tomorrow which they could not yesterday – and *never* have?" Sure, perhaps today's rainbow seems a bit brighter than yesterday's, but it is still just an illusion, with nothing at the end but an empty promise. Today's fascination may have a "new and improved" twist that might thrill for a while in some novel way, but endless experiences prove that the fascination will be short-lived and the emptiness long-lived. What a tragic thing human life would be if there were no answers for our deep hungers! How devastating it would be were we not capable of anything higher than trivial enjoyments!

I have been crucified with Christ and I no longer live, but Christ lives in me. The life I now live in the body, I live by faith in the Son of God, who loved me and gave himself for me. ... May I never boast except in the cross of our Lord

Jesus Christ, through which the world has been crucified to me, and I to the world. (Galatians 2:20; 6:14)

But, my friend, if anyone should know - from bitter experience – of the emptiness of "things" and the inability of this world to satisfy one's deepest longings, it is you. Listening to your story, you have had more than your share of disappointments and worldly heartache. I think that our gracious God has actually been at work in these tough times to wean you from this world and draw you toward Himself. I can see His providential hand in all that you have been walking through. Many things that the world cherishes and dotes upon have proven to be nothing but sources of grief to you, and you have learned that neither your wealth nor your natural advantages are enough to feed and nourish your soul. You have learned (and it is a good lesson to learn!) that every rose has its thorn and every gourd has its worm. Others may see your natural blessing and envy you. But their understanding is shallow. Or, they might pity you for the trials you have walked through, but they do not see a deeper, Divine work taking place.

In your case, if anything in your life has been unbalanced, it has been your love for your friends and family. Your heart is so huge! But I think you have often misplaced your affection and dared to love creatures with love that only God deserves (and can keep safe). Now, ah, it seems that God has removed the dearest of these idols from your life (a severe, but needed mercy), so that you *have to* raise your mind and heart toward Heaven ... where it belongs.

BEGIN BY DOING WHAT GOD COMMANDS

Once we have put our appetites in place, restraining not only our evil desires, but even gaining mastery over our lawful wants (at least in part), there are positive things that we can do to move our hearts forward in loving God. We can actually awaken True Life! It is not some strange magic, but begins with *doing what God has asked of us.* Every day there are choices to make - conscious decisions which honour God, which He has told us to do, and which will incline us toward Life once they get the upper hand in our hearts.

If we are having trouble getting our inner life changed, then we can begin with our outer life. I know that many say that without the heart, the actions are hypocritical, but that is not always the case. The heart can actually follow the actions. It can engage once the actions are engaged. In other words, there may be times when we do our duty, regardless of our hearts, and we find the heart follows the will. If we are not on fire with love towards God, then let's not just be passive and wait. Let's do what we are commanded to do! We can give God our best whether we feel like it or not. We can begin by listening to His Word, both as preached and as we read it. We can praise Him for all His goodness to us. We can speak reverently about Him. We can urge and encourage others to trust and follow Him.

Likewise, if we want hearts of compassion for our neighbours, we must recognize that we can begin by taking every opportunity to do acts of kindness and mercy – regardless of feelings. Don't miss a chance to do good to another, and your heart will one day follow! If you find within you a proud heart, practice servanthood and one day you will find within a servant's heart.

External actions can have value in moving you toward a warm heart. True, the Apostle Paul admits that: "Physical training is of some [little] value," but he does not say it is of *no* value. It is always good and right to do what we can, knowing that God will have mercy on us and help us with even our weak efforts. And, get this: when true love finally does take root in our hearts, it will find the soil there already plowed because of the habits we have been form-ing. Do not worry about being labeled a hypocrite for acting before you are feeling. You know that your goal is not to appear better than you are, but to really become the person your actions are presenting you to be. You know that your actions are coming from a right sense of your duty to God and others, so carry on, without hesitation, knowing that your heart will follow your will!

NEXT, WORK ON YOUR INNER LIFE

As the outward will lead the inward, there are specific things we can do to develop our hearts. These will have a powerful influence for good upon us. Begin by often lifting our hearts to God. If we do not love Him above everything else, then begin by admit-ting it! And let's admit that it is not only our duty, but that we will be finally happy when we do so. Let's lament the dishonor done to our wonderful God by careless men and women everywhere. Let's rejoice whenever He is honoured and praised, and rejoice that He is perfectly praised right now in Heaven. Let's resolve – with joy – to offer up our hearts to Him continually, to live under His Lordship and to serve at His pleasure. And, should our stubborn hearts sputter, stall, and then refuse, let's go back, and say "yes" from where we last said "no." Let's tell our wonderful God again and again that He is good and good to us, that we are convinced that all His ways are right, and that we do truly want Him to do whatever He pleases in, to, and through us – whether we joyfully obey or not!

Now, if we want to see our hearts filled with true love for others, even for everyone, we need to be *deliberately* desiring their happiness, and blessing every person we see. This is supernatural! But, if we earnestly seek grace from God to be filled with universal love for all, He will give it. He can give us all grace to live for the benefit of others, relieving their misery, and desiring their fullness.

> … being confident of this, that he who began a good work in you will carry it on to completion until the day of Christ Jesus. (Philippians 1:6)

This is all exercise for the soul! We are training ourselves for godliness and True Life. When the Spirit of God finds us exercising our own wills and powers to love God and mankind, He is sure to get on board with His power to move the whole endeavor from the natural to the supernatural. *He* will change our hearts. That is a certainty! His wonderful workings within us will follow our ordinary resolve and efforts. As we train our natural powers, His grace will move in us until we find brand new habits of love formed within, flowing from us with a freedom and ease never known before.

> To him who is able to keep you from stumbling and to present you before his glorious presence without fault and with great joy – to the only God our Saviour be glory, majesty, power and authority, through Jesus Christ our Lord, before all ages, now and for evermore! Amen. (Jude 24, 25)

THINKING ABOUT TRUE LIFE DEVELOPS TRUE LIFE

I want to present two other means for developing transformation in the heart. First, there is great value in *thinking* great thoughts about True Life. Opening your Bible, and lifting your heart to Heaven and thinking about things beyond the trivial will do your soul a world of good.

Since, then, you have been raised with Christ, set your hearts on things above, where Christ is, seated at the right hand of God. Set your minds on things above, not on earthly things. (Colossins 3:1-2)

Most of us give little if any thought to things above. Our minds are consumed with the temporary and seen. When we do happen to raise our minds just a little, our thoughts are often foolish and false - more in fashion with the culture around us than with the Truth.

We can be so lazy about spiritual things, unconcerned about the truthfulness of what we think and speak. We are unwilling to contend for Truth and wrestle against the foolish notions of the culture around us. Many around us call themselves "Christian," but are clearly unwilling to think through the implications of Christ upon their lives. Shallow thinking produces shallow living!

Such low, lifeless, paralyzing thoughts are not able to move the hand or the heart. Do the hard work of *thinking* until you are *feeling* and *moved*. "Be still before the Lord and wait patiently for him." (Psalm 37:7).

Ponder and pray and consider until you are fully persuaded of the Truth in regards to things that *matter*. We move away from meaningful meditation too quickly and back to time-wasting trivialities. Stay. Think. Ponder. Pray. Let Truth deeply affect you. Push your soul forward and hold it before the invisible eternal world until it sees clearly that the things we see are transient dreams and the things we cannot see are solid.

So we fix our eyes not on what is seen, but on what is unseen, since what is seen is temporary, but what is unseen is eternal. (2 Corinthians 4:8)

There are ways to help us lift our hearts from the mundane and trivial toward the heavenly and meaningful. First, learn to think from the seen to the unseen and from the temporary to the lasting. When we see the wonder and beauty of this present world, and behold its order and harmony, we can lift our hearts above and beyond the creation and to the Creator. Let us consider the nature, wisdom, and goodness of the One we cannot see who made the wonders we can see.

Then, consider ourselves. We are clearly more than just machines, atoms, and chemicals. We need to lift our thoughts to the wonders of God as we consider the wonders of man. We are currently sluggish, clogged, and marred, but we can still detect the Divine Image within us. There are signs of Life! So, we need to joyfully anticipate a better day when these bodies will be transformed, we will be loosed and we will be with the Lord in a state of Glory currently beyond imagination.

> [Jesus] by the power that enables him to bring everything under his control, will transform our lowly bodies so that they will be like his glorious body. (Philippians 3:21)

> Father, I want those you have given me to be with me where I am, and to see my glory, the glory you have given me because you loved me before the creation of the world. (John 17:24)

Next, when seeing the brokenness and tragedy of this sinful world, when saddened by the wickedness and folly of our race, we can – and must – raise our thoughts and hearts to a place where there will be no more brokenness from sin. There is a world coming whose inhabitants will live in undiluted joy in the very presence of the One they love. There we will – without hindrance - flourish in every way that God first intended. Dwelling upon this future fact will empower us to live transformed lives today.

Look! God's dwelling-place is now among the people, and he will dwell with them. They will be his people, and God himself will be with them and be their God. He will wipe every tear from their eyes. There will be no more death or mourning or crying or pain, for the old order of things has passed away. (Revelation 21:3,4)

Finally, let us always consider Jesus. Why did He come from Heaven to Earth? Didn't he come to take us from Earth to Heaven? Why did He endure death? Was it not to deliver us from death to Life? Why did He know our sorrow? Was it not to bring us His Joy? Our Lord Jesus has Himself opened the Kingdom of Heaven for us and all believers, and He is right now sitting at the right hand of Majesty on High (*c.f.* Hebrews 1:3). There He receives our prayers, intercedes for us before His Father, and grants us grace and help in our worst and most needy times. From Heaven He is pouring out His Holy Spirit upon us to strengthen and encourage us. Certainly the consideration of the wonders of Jesus should move our hearts from low things to higher things.

Who then is the one who condemns? No one. Christ Jesus who died – more than that, who was raised to life – is at the right hand of God and is also interceding for us. Who shall separate us from the love of Christ? Shall trouble or hardship or persecution or famine or nakedness or danger or sword? As it is written:

'For your sake we face death all day long;
we are considered as sheep to be slaughtered.'

No, in all these things we are more than conquerors through him who loved us. (Romans 8:34-37)

CONSIDERING THE HEART OF GOD BIRTHS HIS LOVE IN OUR HEARTS

Taking deliberate and dedicated time to dwell upon the things spoken of above and other truths is the way to see living faith (as opposed to dead religion) birthed in our hearts. And True Life is rooted in living faith.

So, I want to offer some specifics for meditation … things to *think* about in regards to God and His ways. It is when we open our Bibles and discover the ways of God and then dwell upon them with earnest hearts that our inner lives are increasingly transformed.

And we all, who with unveiled faces contemplate the Lord's glory, are being transformed into his image with ever-increasing glory, which comes from the Lord, who is the Spirit. (2 Corinthians 3:18)

First, take time to reflect upon the wonderful nature of God. With your Bible open, study what God is like. God is who He reveals Himself to be in the Bible. God is who He reveals Himself to be in Jesus Christ. We cannot know *everything* about God, but that does not mean we cannot know *many things* about God. And we can know enough to move our hearts. We are more than just creatures of our five senses. The consideration of the nature of God will go beyond what we see and affect our deeper selves.

Just take things on a human level. You have heard of and become in some measure acquainted with some great and wonderful people. It is not a photograph of them that moves you, for your admiration goes way beyond the simple image of them your eyes can give. No, it is the report of their character, their disposition, their wisdom, or their greatness of mind that moves your heart toward them. You have gone where mere senses cannot take you. Now, if such love can grow in your heart where humans are concerned, certainly it can grow in your heart where God is concerned ... if you will simply behold the wonders of God and His nature as revealed in the Bible and all around you.

God in His wonders is infinitely more capable of thrilling our hearts than any creature, if we will just take the time to let Him. His wisdom and goodness are everywhere to be seen. His power and providential care hold the very universe together (*c.f.* Colossian 1:17). The greatest person is but the faintest reflection of God in His perfection. If a person can move us to admiration, how much more should God?

> Before the mountains were born
> or you brought forth the whole world,
> from everlasting to everlasting you are God.
> (Psalm 90: 2)

> The heavens declare the glory of God;
> the skies proclaim the work of his hands.
> (Psalm 19:1)

For in him all things were created: things in heaven and on earth, visible and invisible, whether thrones or powers or rulers or authorities; all things have been created through him and for him. He is before all things, and in him all things hold together. (Colossian 1:16,17)

Is it right that we make so much of our fragmented and imperfect images of God and His glory and so little of God Himself? We dote upon the fallen and broken and yawn at the Perfect and Wonderful. We stare at the imperfect print and ignore the original portrait. Look at it this way: Whatever we find beautiful and praiseworthy in a human or in this world should not captivate us but release us - serve to lift our sights and affections Heavenward. Think: If a *drop* is so sweet, how satisfying must the fountain be? If there is so much to wonder at in a mere beam of light, what must the whole Sun be like?

Remember, God is not distant. Don't allow yourself the weak excuse that God is far away, therefore you cannot and need not pursue Him. " … God did this so that they would seek him and perhaps reach out for him and find him, though he is not far from any one of us. 'For in him we live and move and have our being.' As some of your own poets have said, 'We are his offspring.' " (Acts 17:27, 28). In fact, we cannot open our eyes and look anywhere without seeing evidences of Him. He is all around us! If we but turn His way we will find a willing and eager God, ready to engage, embrace and entertain true and meaningful friendship with us … of which all earthly friendships are but a foretaste. God, the King, speaks of us:

> You have stolen my heart, my sister, my bride;
> you have stolen my heart with one glance of
> your eyes, with one jewel of your necklace.
> (Song of Solomon 4:9)

He loves *us* with the affection of a groom for his bride!

Therefore, since God is willing and ready, let us raise our hopes and our thoughts toward Him. We can actually get a clear understanding of just who He is, because He is a God who has unveiled Himself first in nature, then in His Word, and finally and wonderfully, in Jesus Christ. It is in looking at Jesus (not a Jesus we make up, but the Jesus of the Gospels) that we see what God is like. *God is like Jesus.* So, let us consider, behold, contemplate Christ. "The Son is the radiance of God's glory and the exact representation of his being ..." (Hebrews 1:3). "For in Christ all the fullness of the Deity lives in bodily form ..." (Colossians 2:9). God has been truly, sufficiently, and knowingly revealed in Jesus Christ.

So, present Jesus to yourself! Open your Bible (which is a book about Jesus) and discover Him. Take time and behold His Glory. Read the Gospels and let your soul feast upon Him. There you will see – even though clothed in humanity – the wonders of God and His nature. There we can discover God in ways that nature cannot show us. Study Him. Behold Him. Consider Him. Not in your imagination, but in the sacred Book. And, while you are doing so, the fire will begin to burn.

My heart grew hot within me.
While I meditated, the fire burned.
(Psalm 39:3)

The Word became flesh and made his dwelling among us. We have seen his glory, the glory of the one and only Son, who came from the Father, full of grace and truth. (John 1:14)

WE SHOULD ESPECIALLY MEDITATE UPON THE AMAZING LOVE JESUS HAS FOR US

When thinking about the nature and ways of God, there is no better fuel for the heart than to really consider the love with which God has embraced us in Jesus Christ. Nothing stirs the heart more than discovering that someone loves you! Even if a person who is otherwise unpleasant and unkind shows you an act of love and goodness, you are moved towards him. How much more, then, to learn that the One who is Love itself, who is all Goodness and Beauty, loves *you* with an everlasting love? The Everlasting Majesty of Heaven has a kind affection for us and has proven it upon a cross. Take time and allow this wondrous fact to overcome your spirit, melt your heart, and light it aflame.

The Bible brims over with expressions of God's love for you and me and all mankind. And alongside the Bible we have the proof of God's love for us on display all around us. He gave us our lives, and He graciously preserves them moment by moment. He has placed us in an amazing world, rich in endless ways, and super-abundant in its beauty and supply. What grace! He rains down goodness upon both the good and the bad, and so abundantly supplies our needs that while we are gathering this years' bounty, He is preparing the world for next years'. He then adds sweetness to our lives with friendships and earthly joys far beyond what we deserve and gives us one earthly comfort after another. All this for sinners! He never removes from us His watchful eye. Even when we sleep, He is mindful of us even though we are forgetful of Him.

> He will not let your foot slip –
> he who watches over you will not slumber;
> indeed, he who watches over Israel
> will neither slumber nor sleep.

> The Lord watches over you –
> the Lord is your shade at your right hand;
> (Psalm 121:3-5)

Now I can hear the skeptic's charge: "It is an easy and painless thing for God to display His love in all these ways. What does it cost Him to send rain, and sun, and comfort to His creatures?" Well, He has not only loved us in these ways, but, more wonderfully, He has loved us in suffering. And, since in His Divine nature He could not suffer, He has taken upon Himself our nature, and as Jesus, the Man who is God, He has loved us with unimaginable suffering. The Eternal Son of God, who for all eternity past knew nothing but the unbroken joy of Heaven, emptied Himself and took up human weakness. He came to a people who rejected Him. He lived amongst a rebellious people, and died as a sacrifice and wrath-bearing offering for them.

> He was despised and rejected by mankind,
> a man of suffering, and familiar with pain.
> Like one from whom people hide their faces
> he was despised, and we held him in low esteem.
> (Isaiah 53:3)

You see, at just the right time, when we were still powerless, Christ died for the ungodly. Very rarely will anyone die for a righteous person, though for a good person someone might possibly dare to die. But God demonstrates his own love for us in this: while we were still sinners, Christ died for us. (Romans 5:6-8)

There was a poet once who wonderfully expressed the love of God, as it overcame his own heart, this way: He had long resisted the approaches of God toward him. It seemed as if God had shot all the arrows of His love to his heart, but none had penetrated – until – He put Himself (In the Person of His Son, Jesus) in the bow and shot Himself straight into his heart. This explains the Love of God for us! He has long approached, displayed, and spoken of His love, but when all else fell short, He finally spoke most clearly and proved His love when He made a gift of Himself for us.

> In the past God spoke to our ancestors through the proph-
> ets at many times and in various ways, but in these last
> days he has spoken to us by his Son, whom he appointed
> heir of all things, and through whom also he made the
> universe. The Son is the radiance of God's glory and the
> exact representation of his being, sustaining all things by
> his powerful word. After he had provided purification for
> sins, he sat down at the right hand of the Majesty in heav-
> en. (Hebrews 1:1-3)

The Gospels present the amazing story of the Love of Jesus for this lost world. His condescension, His life of suffering, His poverty, His love for the unloved, His patience with His disciples, His death for sinners - all are undeniable evidences of His love for us. But the Cross! Can there be greater proof of the love of God for sinners? Can there be greater proof of the love of God for *you*? We need to *dwell* upon this, that " … being rooted and established in love, [you] may have power, together with all the Lord's holy people, to grasp how wide and long and high and deep is the love of Christ, and to know this love that surpasses knowledge – that you may be filled to the measure of all the fullness of God." (Ephesians 3:17-19)

For God so loved the world that he gave his one and only Son, that whoever believes in him shall not perish but have eternal life. For God did not send his Son into the world to condemn the world, but to save the world through him. (John 3:16,17)

In light of the amazing Love of God proven with Jesus on the cross, we should often stop and think of the unending patience of God for us – we who have been so slow to repent, so in love with our sins and foolishness. God has poured goodness and mercy upon us while we have wrestled against Him time and again. He has contended in love with our stubbornness (while He could have cast us off) using endless methods to recover us when we did not want to be recovered. What Love!

It would do our hearts immeasurable good to journal the blessings God has bestowed upon us. We would then see plainly that things are not just "chance" occurrences, but the distinct fingerprints of the hand of our gracious God upon us. We would clearly see answers to specific prayers. And, seeing the abundant goodness of God in our lives, we dare not, for a minute, think that God is being manipulative by pouring goodness upon us only to increase His case against us for damning us later. No! God is not cagey and shifty like we are! His love for us is pure and without any ill-motive. He only desires our repentance and grateful hearts. God desires that none of His creatures perish (*c.f.* 2 Peter 3:9). If we abuse His generosity and plunge ourselves into greater guilt, that is our doing, not His design.

Once these considerations bring us to a deeper affection toward God, all the other branches of True Life will, as a matter of course, grow and prosper.

TO HAVE LOVE IN OUR HEARTS FOR OTHERS, WE MUST REMEMBER THAT ALL PEOPLE ARE DIVINE IMAGE BEARERS

We will find love in our hearts for others growing as we remember and consider the fact that *all* people are stamped with the image of God and are as nearly related to Him as we are ourselves. Like us, they are not only His creatures, "fearfully and wonderfully made" (Psalm 139:14), but, also like us, are the recipients of His special care. For them, too, God has an eternal design for good, planned from the foundations of the world and extending into Eternity. Think of the most miserable and offensive person you know. He is as loved by God as you are. He is the offspring of Heaven as well. No matter how unworthily he might present himself, he deserves our warm embrace and true affection as surely as does any noble and upright friend.

Think about how you regard someone who is closely related to one whom you love. The love you have for your friend cascades upon those who are related to him. We all will gladly take any chance to bless the child of a friend. We do it in large part because we know that we will bless the friend as we bless his child. Without question, if we simply considered the nearness of all people to the God who loves us, we would treat them in ways that bring blessing to the God we claim to love. Love would naturally spring from our hearts to others. It will do us well to ponder the fact that every soul, *every* soul, is dearer to God than all the universe, and that He did not spare His own Son in securing its redemption from sin.

My friend, at the risk of repeating myself, even people in their fallen condition bear the image of God, though marred (see Genesis 6:9). This should move us to love them. Imagine! The very image of the One who loved us first is stamped upon all people we meet. If we cannot love them for their sake, certainly we can love them for

His sake. In some, that image is comparatively easy to see; in others it is so obscured by sin that it is hard to find, but even then it has not been obliterated.

Every person we meet is a rational and immortal soul. Every person is capable of wonderful thinking, amazing creativity, and, by grace, God-glorifying living. It may be that sin has him in bondage for now, and his faculties are marred and diminished. But this should move our compassion, not extinguish our love. When we see someone terribly distorted and captured by sin, consumed by evil and foolishness, we admit that it is hard to love such a person. But, right then, we need to remember that this twisted soul is actually capable of the highest thought, wisdom, and goodness. Just a drop of God's grace is enough to transform a wretch into a creature as noble as the greatest saint. That person – now so distorted by sin – can by grace be a fit companion for the angels of Heaven. In fact, that is the story of many throughout history! Remembering this can and should turn our disposition toward him from bitter to sweet, from disdain to pity. If you saw a beautiful body ruined by some physical tragedy, you would not stand in judgment, but be moved to pity and to action on his behalf. However much we might and should hate his crimes and sins, we should pity and love him. The highest rule of love is given to us from Jesus Himself: "My command is this: love each other as I have loved you." (John 15:12)

THE DIGNITY OF OUR NATURE SHOULD INSPIRE US TO LOVE PURITY

How we view ourselves, as people made in the image of God, is vital to the life-choices we make. If we see ourselves merely as "animals", even "higher" animals, we will live to feed our lower natures. We will starve our souls. If we misjudge our natures, we will sink into a love of sensual pleasures and self-gratification. If we are animals, why not behave like animals? But we are *not* animals. We are the pinnacle of God's creation, made in God's Image. And, if we will love our souls, and seek to purify them and disentangle them from this world, we need to know who and whose we are! For all of our sin and fallen-ness, we need to know and rejoice in the dignity and excellence of our nature. Otherwise, we will feed the beast and starve the Christian!

If we know and consider who we are, and the grand purpose for which we have been created – to know, enjoy, and glorify God – then we will (in a right way) stand in awe of ourselves. Understanding that we are Divine Image bearers will at the same time produce a holy reverence for ourselves and all others, and a holy modesty towards ourselves and others. It will cause us to have a reserve and thankfulness in the use of the good things that God has given us to enjoy, and a hatred of things which God forbids, because they will sicken our souls.

LEARN TO THINK ABOUT HEAVEN

If we can learn to consider Heaven, we will find our hearts being stirred, warmed, and weaned from worldliness. If we learn to do this every day, presenting to our minds the Bible's descriptions of Heaven's eternal pleasures, we will find a transforming power for godliness; a power enabling us to defeat sin.

> Dear friends, now we are children of God, and what we will be has not yet been made known. But we know that when Christ appears, we shall be like him, for we shall see him as he is. All who have this hope in him purify themselves, just as he is pure. (1 John 3:2-4)

We will live like "strangers and pilgrims" (Hebrews 11:13) here if we are often thinking about our true and final home. We will find power over the lure of our own lusts and the world's enticements. We will find the chains easier to break when our heads are lifted and our hope is fixed above. We will gladly keep ourselves from being spoiled by this world when our joy is fixed upon the next.

It is vital that we view Heaven rightly. We are not speaking of the sensual paradise of the Muslim. Nor are we to use the Bible in some vulgar way, abusing its images to present a paradise that is merely a feast for the senses (Although our senses will certainly be enlivened there!). Heaven is Heaven because God – Father, Son, and Spirit – is there.

So! When we begin to see Heaven as the dwelling place of God, and our invitation is to be with Him forever, "beholding His glory'" (John 17:24), then we can go ahead and fill our minds with every good thought of our future blessedness. And, when we do so, how small and undesirable do the things that currently captivate us become! Sin will become contemptible in our eyes: "How dare this momentary pleasure threaten to keep me from Eternal Joy!" With force we can rebuke those gross and muddy pleasures that are trying to rob us of True Life and Eternal Happiness, and render us unfit for God's grand design for us.

By faith Moses, when he had grown up, refused to be known as the son of Pharaoh's daughter. He chose to be ill-treated along with the people of God rather than to enjoy the fleeting pleasures of sin. He regarded disgrace for the sake of Christ as of greater value than the treasures of Egypt, because he was looking ahead to his reward. By faith he left Egypt, not fearing the king's anger; he persevered because He saw him who is invisible. (Hebrews 11:24-27)

BEING AWARE OF OUR FAILINGS HELPS HUMILITY GROW WITHIN US

Many - if not most - of us have seasons where we entertain conceited and proud views of ourselves. These seasons may last for a few moments … perhaps in the midst of an argument … or for years. But here is where our very failures and sins can actually *help* us. Our foolishness, when faced and admitted, can actually be used to pull down our walls of pride and conceit.

When people esteem us, more often than not it is because they see some small virtue in us, but do not see the large evil in us. They see some good, but miss much that is bad. If they knew us more thoroughly they would quickly change their minds about us.

The thoughts and motives of our hearts *on our best days*, if paraded before all the world to see, would make us look anything but holy and full of virtue. People would either dislike us, shun us, or think us ridiculous. Now, you can conceal yourself from others, at least to some degree, but if you honestly appraise yourself, you will see the bad parts that others miss. Seeing them will expose your vanity. Godly men and women the world over will tell us that they are far more aware of their own sins than those of others. They know their own hearts well, and, like the Apostle Paul, consider themselves to be the worst of sinners.

> Here is a trustworthy saying that deserves full acceptance: Christ Jesus came into the world to save sinners – of whom I am the worst. (1 Timothy 1:15)

Godly people are much more concerned with the beam in their own eye, than they are with the speck in their brother's. And, being so self-aware, that knowledge promotes humility of heart and manner.

THINKING RIGHTLY ABOUT GOD LEADS TO THINKING RIGHTLY ABOUT OURSELVES

While considering our own failings can certainly help us toward humility, there is still a better way to grow a humble nature: Considering the greatness of God. Yes we need to be aware of, and even at times mournfully dwell upon, our own failures. But a deep and quiet contemplation of the goodness and beauty of God will do more to produce true humility is us. Our blemishes never appear so obvious as when they are exposed in His perfect light. When we look down upon ourselves from His vantage, we see our smallness. We then see clearly that we have been measuring ourselves by the false standard of men instead of the right standard of God. Humility born of a view of our sinfulness can be more or less turbulent as it can strangely be mixed with self-righteousness, ("I am ashamed of myself!") but humility born of a knowledge of God's nature lays us truly low, with no room for a drop of self, and actually brings a deep peace to our hearts.

THE VALUE AND WORTH OF PRAYER TO TRUE LIFE

There is still another means of developing the inner life: Regular and fervent prayer.

God has promised His Holy Spirit to us. And, by the atoning work of Jesus He has opened a clear way to the Throne of Grace. We can pray! I am not sure if we understand the wonder of this! We, mere creatures of dust, but more, bearers of the very Image of God - fallen, then redeemed by the blood of Jesus - can approach the Holy Holy Holy God of the Universe! When we pray, we open ourselves up to the influences of Heaven. It is then that the Lord, the "sun of righteousness," (*c.f.* Malachi 4:2) can visit us with the most direct rays of His love. It is then that He can dispel our darkness and do His deepest work in our souls.

There are many books written on prayer. I do not need to write one here. It is sufficient just to say that there are different types of prayer. First there is vocal prayer. We speak out in words. Obviously this is what we do when we pray in public or with others, and sometimes it is helpful to pray out loud in private.

Then, there is prayer where we do not make a sound at all. We are communicating with the Lord in silence and secret, in our minds and in our thoughts.

But, ah ... there is a third and yet more wonderful kind of prayer. In this the soul flies higher. It has long meditated on issues, and Truth, and God's nature, and man's plight, and as a result if fires like a rocket – full of purpose, direction, and heat – to the very Throne of Grace. Here there are sighs and groans beyond words, beyond the capabilities of any human expression. After a time of deep and meaningful contemplation of the nature and attributes of God, as seen in all His wonderful works in nature and in the Gospel, the heart pours itself out to its God in the deepest adoration and worship. Following a season of brokenness over sin, and sad awareness of its vileness and corruption, the heart falls before its Holy God, daring not to speak a word or lift an eye to Heaven. It is desperately aware of its urgent need of grace. Having dwelt upon the true beauty of holiness and the happiness of those who have sought hard after God and who have put off sin, the heart thirsts for God alone and prays with such desire that words cannot be found - not just for a moment but for a season as it finds itself upheld by the power of its own deep desire.

This kind of "deep soul prayer" is perhaps more than anything else the most powerful purifier for the soul. It seems to go beyond words, and engages directly with the Spirit of God: "In the same way, the Spirit helps us in our weakness. We do not know what we ought to pray for, but the Spirit himself intercedes for us through wordless groans." (Romans 8:26) Praying in this way is one of the most powerful means of obtaining True Life and one of the most effective weapons in the Christian's arsenal.

(Just a warning: Such deep prayer is not the only type of effective praying! In fact the sighings and heavings that accompany such praying require such time and energy that we cannot pray this way all the time. There is also great effectiveness in simply praying with your voice, in gatherings with others, or silently in your own heart. But, without question, the type of prayer spoken of above will do great good for your soul.)

TRUE LIFE WILL BE GREATLY AIDED BY PARTAKING OF HOLY COMMUNION

My dear friend, before I leave you I want to encourage you in one more way. The Lord Jesus has given us something simple, but very sacred, in the Sacrament of Holy Communion. Bread and Wine. Not magic, but so powerful to nourish the soul. Jesus Christ has given this so that, when we use it conscientiously, our souls are fed and made strong.

There is not a more potent reminder of the Atonement than these two elements that together form one Sacrament. When done righty, reverently, and thoughtfully, we are made to dwell upon all the benefits of Jesus' life and death for us. In a real sense, all spiritual disciplines converge in this one sacred act. It is during Communion that we (should) take the most serious look at our lives, both inward and outward. It is then that we focus our minds on things above, and on the gracious and holy character of our God. It is then that we can make the greatest and most important decisions about our lives. It is then that we repent, believe, and resolve. It is then that we renew both our contempt for the world and our love for those in it. It is then that we receive afresh the wonders of the death of Christ for our sins. It is then that we are renewed, refreshed, and reconsecrated to the Lord and His Kingdom. It is then that we make our boldest approach – even assault - to Heaven and to Heaven's Throne.

FINAL PRAYER

And now, my friend, it is time to close this letter. I am afraid it has grown longer than I intended! But it is my hope that this simple effort will bring some good to your soul and lead you in your desire for True Life. If that be the case, then how happy I will be! So, I trust that you will accept this little work of mine, that I might in some small way fulfill my happy duty to be a blessing to you.

Now, if I can close with an earnest prayer to the Lord, the Hope of our Souls.

"Our Good and Gracious God! Thank You for putting into our hearts a desperate desire for True Life. We bless you for making us discontented with all the empty and trivial things of this passing world. We ask You please, to ignite our hearts with such an ardent desire for Yourself, and for things that will last, so that we will apply all diligence and patience to this pursuit of Life. Deliver us from trusting in our own strength, but also deliver us from being lazy … waiting for You to do what you have commanded *us* to do. Empower us to do our best even as we trust in You and depend upon You for success in our pursuit of True Life.

Open our eyes to wonderful things in your Word. Give life to our consciences so that we will see and hate sin and everything that would harm our souls and bring You sadness and dishonor. Cause us to love what You love and hate what You hate! Take ownership of our hearts, Lord. And in owning us, give us a holy disdain for things that used to captivate us and trick us into thinking they could give us Life. Turn our eyes away from vain things and to Your Wonderful Self.

In the place of foolish things, fill us with a wonder and sense of You and Your Truths that will last. May the things which You have revealed in the Bible captivate us and influence every part of our lives, to the end that this life which we now live in these lowly bodies, we will live through faith in Jesus, and for His Glory.

Live Your Life in us, Lord!

Lord! May the infinite wonder of You fill our hearts! May Your astonishing Goodness and Love overwhelm every part of who we are! Come and conquer our hearts, that they might be constantly rising to You in the flames of true devotion and desperate pursuit. Enlarge our hearts with true love for every soul in this fallen world. Fill us with a tender affection for others, even those who offend You with their every breath. Move on us that we might be cleansed from every filthy thought and deed, that we might rightly revere You and grow in holiness of heart and life – without which we can never hope to see You and enjoy You.

Finally, Lord, may a true knowledge of Yourself and of ourselves … Your Wonderful Nature and our fallen nature (though marvelously made in Your Image) both serve to humble and silence us and stir us toward Yourself in earnest desire for You and True Life in You. We here happily resign ourselves to Your Holy Spirit that He may lead us into all Truth and impart into us True Life.

Wonderful God of our salvation, guide us with Your tender counsel. And after, receive us into Your Glorious Presence, by the Merits of Your Dear Son, our Saviour, Jesus Christ.

We are Yours!

Amen"

Closing Thoughts and an Invitation to True Life

~

… God has chosen to make known … the glorious riches
of this mystery, which is Christ in you, the hope of glory.
(Colossians1:27)

HENRY SCOUGAL'S LETTER TO HIS friend ended as abruptly as it began.
Again, there were no wasted words in this dying man, no excess to
trim. He has presented – not only to his friend but to you and me –
the supernatural life, True Life, which God designs for every believer
in Jesus. What Scougal makes wonderfully plain is that this supernatural life is not an esoteric, secret, spooky life for a few select mystics.
This is not Gnosticism, but plain, real, God-originated *Christianity*. It
is the union of the gracious Saviour and the needy sinner. It is Christ
indwelling the humble, plain believer. There are no séances, but there
are Bible studies; no fortunes told, but there is living faith in the Bible's
God. It is a mystery *revealed*, an open invitation to a willing God.

I think after reading Scougal I am left without an excuse. I am as
holy – and therefore as happy – as I want to be. True Life is not complicated, but it is challenging. It is simple, but not always easy. I have to get
to a place of desperation. I have to get to that precious soul-place where
I realize that Jesus is my only Hope, and where all else bows before Him

and takes its rightful place. When there, I am on the brink of Life, on the front porch of the Father's House. If I miss out on True Life, it is because I wanted less, not more; I was too easily satisfied with husks; I treasured lesser gods above the only True God.

Scougal's thesis: *The health and well-being of your soul is determined and measured by the value of that which you love the most,* is both a challenge and a warm invitation. It is a challenge to leave off all lesser loves, and an invitation to love Jesus Christ supremely. The assurance here is that we will find a willing God in all of this. We need never fear that in leaving all idols behind we will not find a welcoming God in their stead. Scougal's God – the Bible's God – has designed us for Himself, and redeemed us through the Blood of Christ for Himself, and for nothing less.

So, let us fear not and press in! Let us refuse to be satisfied with mere right belief, or right living, or right feeling (as important as these are). Let us be satisfied with nothing short of that for which Christ has redeemed us: That we should know God, Father, Son, and Spirit, in our hearts and experience. That Christ would be found dwelling within us, even as we are found hidden in Him. Then, when He has become more precious to us than all others, sin will be as abhorrent to us as cancer. The veil between this brief life and Eternity will become wondrously thin, and we shall find ourselves living in the suburbs of Heaven.

I have been crucified with Christ and I no longer live, but Christ lives in me. The life I now live in the body, I live by faith in the Son of God, who loved me and gave himself for me. (Galatians 2:20)

Yours for True Life,

John Gillespie

25298819R00087

Printed in Great Britain
by Amazon